THE LIST

THE LIST

FIGURING OUT PRINCE CHARMING,
THE CORNER OFFICE, AND HAPPILY EVER AFTER

Marian Jordan

B&H
PUBLISHING GROUP
Nashville. Tennessee

978-0-8054-4671-5

Published by B&H Publishing Group

Nashville, Tennessee

Dewey Decimal Classification: 248.843

Subject Heading: CHRISTIAN LIFE \ WOMEN \

YOUNG WOMEN

1 2 3 4 5 6 7 8 • 13 12 11 10 09

Dedication

This book is lovingly dedicated to my precious friend
and mentor in Christ, Tonya Riggle.
Thank you for choosing God's List.
I've learned what it means to glorify God,
to seek first the kingdom, and to dance with Jesus
because of your faithful example.
Truly, you are a woman after God's own heart.

Table of Contents

The List

This is your life, are you who you want to be?
—SWITCHFOOT

My girlfriends were given strict instructions:

No party.
No gifts.
No balloons.
No singing.
No cake.
And definitely, no candles!

Like harsh daylight to the sleep deprived, candles were a glaring and dreaded reminder of the very thing I was hoping to forget ... my big-fat-incredibly-horrible ... birthday.

You see, I was desperately trying to ignore my birthday. Ignore is quite the understatement; amnesia would have been welcomed!

Toward this goal, I plotted a clever (if I do say so myself) escape-the-horrid-birthday-blues strategy. No, I didn't drink myself into a drunken stupor. No, I didn't max out my credit card. No, I didn't invite my friends Ben and Jerry over for a weekend of comfort bingeing. My idea was sober, slimming, and oh-so-cunning. Genius, really. I surmised: *If I quietly leave town and don't allow anyone to throw the usual birthday bash, then I can simply pretend like that frightful day isn't happening. Then maybe, just maybe, I won't have to face the crushing reality that I am yet another year older.*

Like I said—brilliant.

Right?

The boycott-my-birthday plan took shape, and I jetted off to a faraway destination with "woe is me" as my anthem and a knot in my stomach so large I feared I would be charged for extra baggage. The plan was perfect. Perfect, that is, until I boarded the plane and realized I'd taken myself with me. Girls, here's a word of advice (and this one's for free): it doesn't matter where you go or how far you try to run, your problems always go with you.

So, what was *my* problem?

Why was I dreading the arrival of my birthday like the arrival of a maxed-out credit card bill? Normally, I'm a party girl—oh, in the Christian sense of the word, of course. I'm all about a celebration. I L-O-V-E the cake, the confetti, the candles, the no-really-you-shouldn't-have birthday treats . . . the total girly giddiness of being the birthday girl.

But not this year. Instead, I shrank from the limelight that

2

came with being queen for the day. Instead I wanted to slip off into anonymity and hide from the spotlight. You see, I'd just endured a brutally tough season on the personal front, one that I called the wilderness, and my looming age change had the potential to send me scurrying back into the wild. Therefore, I didn't even want to acknowledge my birthday, much less celebrate it.

I found denial to be a lovely option.

My angst wasn't about getting *older* per se—my anguish was more the result of unmet expectations. I always imagined my life would look different by this age. So instead of being a cause for celebration, my approaching birthday was now a cause for mourning. It screamed at me, mocked me, and tortured me with its looming largeness. And somehow, the most powerful emotion I experienced in those days wasn't fear or sadness—it was shame. Shame? Yes, if I am flat-out honest with you, I must admit that I was horrifically embarrassed. I felt like something was terribly wrong with me because my life didn't turn out like my expectations. I was single . . . and this was NOT my plan. I felt like a big failure and a total loser because I hadn't met certain criteria I had set for myself back in junior high.

Yep, I said junior high. Remember those painfully awkward years of braces, growth spurts, and hormone surges? It was then as a wise and mentally stable teenager that I formed the expectations for how my adult life would turn out.

I can picture it now—my thirteenth birthday party. Girls, this was not just any party, this was a slumber party. Oh yes. We

3

thought we were so cool renting *Grease* and watching Michael Jackson's *Thriller* video over and over. By this point, I was definitely aware of the fact that boys did not have cooties, and I was absolutely IN LOVE WITH Rick Springfield. I know, I know, who wasn't?

The evening consisted of slumber party basics: consuming large quantities of pizza and Coca-Cola (not that awful New Coke, of course), toilet-papering houses,* prank-calling boys,** practicing our best Valley girl lingo,*** and "like" the totally most important event of them all, creating the List.

Don't sit there reading this and pretend you, too, haven't created the List. Perhaps your denial is more a case of confusion than it is an outright disagreement. Let's say for argument's sake, you are confused about this thing called the List. Please allow me the honor of refreshing your memory.

---

* Toilet-papering, aka wrapping houses. This activity consists of girls throwing toilet paper onto the trees and lawn of the home of the cute boy in school or their favorite teacher.

** For those of you born after 1985, I must explain a rather important event that occurred in my lifetime. This is the invention of caller ID. Prior to caller ID a girl could call and hang up on her "crush" or ex-boyfriend and no one would be the wiser. But with the invention of said device (from Satan), the fun of the prank call was quickly destroyed for thirteen-year-olds throughout the world.

*** The term *Valley girl* originally referred to rich teenage girls and young women living in the neighborhoods of the San Fernando Valley area of Los Angeles, California. Val is the shorthand form of the term. During the 1980s the term metamorphosed into a caricature of such women: a "ditzy" or "airhead" personality. In Valley girl lingo, the word *like* is often repeated and has several different meanings depending on the context.

The List goes by many names. Some may call it the big life plan, or in some circles it has been known as the what-I'm-gonna-do-when-I-grow-up agenda. However we title it, at some point in our formative years, every one of us made our own List.

I know I made mine. With a gaggle of junior high girls gathered in my parents' living room, we discussed the all-important issues of body development and boys, danced along with Danny and Sandy, and fantasized about our marvelous futures. We had BIG plans . . . and my plan went a little something like this:

> *Number 1.* When I'm sixteen, I'm going to start driving. I'll get my license and a fabulous car. Look out Lufkin (Lufkin, Texas, that is, the small town where I and the List originated).

> *Number 2.* I will graduate from high school. FREEDOM! And I do mean freedom . . . from parents, from acne, from bad-hair days, from mean girls, and from bathrooms shared with multiple siblings. I always knew that if I could just get out of Dodge, everything about me would change. Sudden metamorphosis. Hello? Have you ever seen an ugly sorority girl? So, armed with my high school diploma, a clean slate, and a sunny new outlook . . . oh, the places I could go.

> *Number 3.* Then I will go to the college of my choice, in an exciting location, where I will make lifelong friends. I, of course, will pledge a sorority. Make the dean's list. Meet and date the big man on campus.

Become sweetheart of his fraternity. Get pinned. And make my parents proud as my father escorts me onto the football field as homecoming queen of the university. Good times.

Number 4. After graduation, I will land a killer job and work on my fabulous career. And though my college sweetheart will beg me to marry him, I'll say, "I'm way too focused on my career right now, I can't even think about marriage until I'm at least twenty-four." We break up. And this breaks the poor chap's heart.

Number 5. I meet Mr. Right. Oh, I wasn't looking of course. Actually, I was running from all of my eligible pursuers. But, well, one evening at a charity gala, the host of the event asks *me* to dance. Cinderella would be so proud. The evening takes on a magical quality. He is handsome but not pretty. Very successful and very wealthy but not spoiled. After all, we meet at a charity thing. He pursues. I struggle with the thought of giving up my career that I had worked so hard for, but . . .

Number 6. THE RING! Lovely, the envy of all of my friends, but meaningful to me because . . . well, I designed it. So we are officially engaged! Again, bittersweet, because I, now the blushing bride, have to quit my fabulous, hard-earned career to plan this HUGE wedding.

Number 7. After the wedding of my dreams, we want to take time for "just us," so we travel . . . a lot. I am sadly unable to return to work as I am spending time decorating our new home, where before the ripe old age of thirty I am blessed with two beautiful children, a boy and a girl, respectively. Oh, and don't worry. Though I am a wife and mother, I still take time for my girlfriends (you know, the "lifelong friends" I made in college). You see, for my thirtieth birthday, my husband surprises me with a girls' trip to a tropical location. He flies us all there where we relax and reminisce about our lives, our loves, and our Lists, and how very complete they are.

That was *my* List.

But here's the thing: Life didn't go according to plan Marian. Well, to be fair, some of the things on my List did happen. I *do* in fact have my driver's license. (I'm still not sure how I passed that test.) And, yes, I *do* have several diplomas hanging in my study, but the rest of my List remains unchecked.

Confession time. I'm a single girl well past her self-imposed marriage deadline of twenty-four. And that, my friend, brings us back to the big-fat-ugly birthday I was hoping to ignore. And the List? Well, that sucker began tormenting me in the preceding weeks. Spoken or unspoken, written or unwritten, the List haunts us all in some shape or form. My misery was because there were so many things on my List that weren't checked off.

Meet Mr. Right . . . unchecked

Fairy-tale engagement . . . unchecked

Disgustingly over-the-top wedding . . . unchecked

Perfect, well-behaved kids . . . *you get the picture.*

All of those things were still unchecked. It was just me, my unadorned hand, and my growing fear of spinsterhood.

Therefore, I developed my *new* plan—DENIAL. (Always a great way to deal with a difficult situation.) I decided to just pretend it wasn't happening. So the morning of the big day I boarded a plane. Found my seat. Closed my eyes, and prayed my guts out for time to move backward. Popping one eye open, I peeked to see if I was suddenly thrust back into 1988. I sighed deeply as I saw a flight attendant pushing the beverage cart my way. I guess time travel only works for Michael J. Fox. (Note to self: Next time board a DeLorean instead of a 747.)

There in seat 15E, thirty-five thousand feet above the earth, I did the best thing I could have done for myself—I laughed at my own craziness. Laughter is good . . . freeing really. Honestly, I needed to laugh because I was acting so silly. Here's the truth: I am content, normally. Until that season, I hadn't really struggled with singleness all that much. Sure, I wouldn't have minded meeting Mr. Right, but I wasn't at all desperate to change my status. Even though I'd experienced a few breakups and meltdowns along the way, I was at peace with the fact that God had my time in his hands. And besides all that, I recognized the fact that I have a great life: I've got amazing friends and family, I've traveled the world, and I absolutely love my job. Truly, I had nothing, absolutely nothing, to complain about. I knew I was blessed. But for some reason the age change and obvious lack of check marks on *my* List were sending me spiraling into a pit of fear, shame, and despair.

Realizing all of this, I took advantage of the long cross-country flight to spend some time talking to Jesus about my situation. I'd already learned the hard lesson about pity parties (i.e., Satan's ploy to rob us of our joy and peace). So as I sat there praying and reflecting on my life and present state of singleness, I sensed the Lord speak to me these words of Scripture: "Everything is beautiful in its time."

Remembering the context of this verse, I flipped my Bible open to the third chapter of Ecclesiastes and read:

> There is a time for everything,
> and a season for every activity under heaven:
> a time to be born and a time to die,
> a time to plant and a time to uproot,
> a time to kill and a time to heal,
> a time to tear down and a time to build,
> a time to weep and a time to laugh,
> a time to mourn and a time to dance,
> a time to scatter stones and a time to gather them,
> a time to embrace and a time to refrain,
> a time to search and a time to give up,
> a time to keep and a time to throw away,
> a time to tear and a time to mend,
> a time to be silent and a time to speak,

a time to love and a time to hate,
a time for war and a time for peace.

He [God] has made *everything* beautiful in its time.
(vv. 1–8, 11 NIV, emphasis mine)

OK, so I'm not a total nitwit. I understood the message and how it applied to my particular pity party . . . singleness is a season. There is a time for everything . . . blah, blah, blah, blah. It's not like there aren't four zillion books out there for single women saying all the same thing. So naturally my response was, Yes, yes, Lord, I know, but *how* do I make this season beautiful? Because if I'm going to be honest with you, the way I'm going right now is not so pretty. I need some serious help. You know . . . the supernatural—part the waters, food from ravens—kind of help. And in that emotional state of disappointment mingled with desire I heard the Lord's response to my question. He said, Marian, you need to exchange your List for my List.

Exchange my List? But we've been together for so long. What could this mean?

In the months following that flight I grew to understand more and more what the Lord meant by this exchange. My eyes were opened to see that my List was simply the worldly possessions, accomplishments, and goals I hoped and believed would bring joy and happiness to my life. But as I began to look around, I noticed an amazing truth—there were millions of women out there with their own Lists, and guess what—they really weren't that happy or content either. You can be married *and* miserable. You can climb the corporate ladder and feel nothing but despair at the top. You can have the American dream and feel like you're living a nightmare. The secret to joy in *any* season of life is exchanging our Lists for his List.

This book is all about his List—the biblical truths I've learned that make any season of life beautiful.

Married or single.

College student or senior citizen.

Mommy or CEO.

Bridesmaid or bride.

I've discovered that joy is not found in some future state; it is available now for those of us willing to make the exchange.

> *The life of faith is lived one day at a time, and it has to be lived not always looked forward to as though the real living were around the next corner. It is today for which we are responsible. God still owns tomorrow.*
>
> —Elisabeth Elliot

Shine

To make your season beautiful, become a girl who lives for the glory of God.

We will shine like stars in the universe,
Holding out Your truth in the darkest place.
We'll be living for Your glory!
—MATT REDMAN

Bridezilla

Emerging from a sea of lace and tulle, crushing bridesmaids in her wake, a force comes forth more deadly than a lizard famed to be thirty stories high. She is to be respected. She is to be feared. She is to have the perfect shade of "hot-but-not-Barbie-or-too-baby-pink" nail polish to match her color scheme. She is Bridezilla. And you better believe it, she will be the center of attention. She will SHINE!

OK. So here's what I can't figure out: Why in the world would a sane woman knowingly volunteer to appear on a TV show called *Bridezillas*? The title alone should tell a girl that she's not going to be cast in the most flattering light. It's not like a bride could call "foul" and claim she was tricked by the producers. I'm just sayin', I've known a few Bridezillas in my day, but most of them would quickly deny being one. But not these girls. On the contrary, these 'zillas actually take pride in being vain, selfish, egotistical, and the nightmare of their friends and family. In the series, the women not only *know* they are behaving like monsters, but actually relish the fact that they are getting a little TV time because of their antics.

In case you didn't figure it out from the title, *Bridezilla* is a reality TV show that follows brides-to-be as they plan, prep, and prey on innocent wedding planners for their big day. These girls blatantly admit that the wedding is not about a God-honoring covenant between bride and groom, but instead the ceremony is *her* moment to shine. Finally, it is their time to be the center of attention and pity the fool who would dare stand in their way. These Bridezillas will be made "much of" and they *will* be exalted . . . for the duration of the wedding festivities, so they fight, complain, and cry should anyone have the audacity to forget that it's "all about the bride."

Oh, the drama!

Bridezilla is not alone. Reality TV land is littered with folks crying out for their time in the spotlight. MTV has spawned an entire generation of fame seekers with programs like *My Super Sweet 16* and *MADE*. *My Super Sweet 16* takes viewers on a wild ride behind the scenes for all the drama, surprises, and over-the-top fun as girls prepare for their "most important coming-of-age celebrations." Like Bridezillas, these teens expect and will only accept the absolute best. This series gives you an up close and very personal look at the extravagant and always extreme measures that some teens take to ensure that this milestone in their lives is commemorated by the ultimate celebration. After all, aren't they entitled to their moment of glory?

Ahem . . .

At the heart of these shows are people clamoring for attention. To be seen. To be known. To be made . . . "much of." A generation that cut its teeth on self-esteem classes at school and lived in a world where "everyone is a winner" has emerged as a group that believes everyone is entitled to her fifteen minutes of fame, and some of them (and us) will do anything, literally *anything,* to get it.

I Wanna Be Famous!

A few years ago I attended a dinner honoring graduating high school seniors. At the conclusion of the meal, the parents presented

a video that included cute pictures of the students from their tod-
dler days (you know, when *everyone* was adorable) as well as a
short interview with each graduate in which he or she answered the
question: Where do you see yourself when you're thirty?

I thought to myself, "Oh, this is going to be so good."
Considering the fact that I was nearing the big 3-0 mark myself,
I was eager to hear where these oh-so-wise graduates envisioned life
would take them by the decrepit old age of thirty. The video did
not disappoint.

Here's a snippet of the responses (enjoy).

- "Before I'm thirty I will be a *famous* film producer, and,
  of course, be fabulously wealthy."
- "Before I'm thirty, I will play college football and then
  go on to play for the NFL, where I will be the *star*
  running back."
- "Before I'm thirty, I will write my first best-selling novel,
  which will be adapted quickly into a screenplay that will
  make me *the darling* of Hollywood."
- "Before I'm thirty, I will be a *well-known* recording
  artist, and my first project will be platinum!"

And so on and so on. All but two of the seventy students
included some type of fame on their Lists of accomplishments
before the age of thirty.

The interview responses remind me of the Pussycat Dolls' hit
song "When I Grow Up." In this dance single, the girls confess that

their life aspirations include driving nice cars, having groupies, and getting their faces on TV and in magazines. In a recent interview, lead singer Nicole Scherzinger said "When I Grow Up" is all about fulfilling her childhood wish list.

> All of us started with a dream. I know when I was young, and I would sign people's notebooks, I wrote, "Remember me when I'm famous," and I don't know of a little kid who hasn't aspired to be someone. . . . The lyrics go, "When I grow up, I wanna be famous, I wanna be a star . . ."[1]

Unfiltered, blunt honesty. You gotta love it. Clearly, if there is a list, and obviously there is one, near the top it would read, "When I grow up, I want to be famous."

She is not alone.

Why are so many of us obsessed with fame? Why do we clamor for the spotlight? Why do we desire our name in lights? For one thing, we live in a culture that screams at us to make much of ourselves. To crave attention, to fight for the limelight, to be the one who's watched, applauded, and praised. And the other factor is the desire "to be someone." And clearly, our culture tells us, "You aren't someone unless you're famous."

> **We live in a culture that screams at us to make much of ourselves.**

But is this right? Is fighting for our share of the spotlight *why* we were made?

Why We Were Made

To understand why, we first must recognize the fact that we are, indeed, "made." Created. Formed. Designed. Planned. Fashioned. We are not self-existent creatures. We did not create ourselves. We are the purposeful design of One who is the Creator of all things. The Author of life. The holy, awesome, and majestic God of the universe. The Bible says, "God made man in His own likeness. . . . He made both male and female. . . . He breathed into his nose the breath of life. Man became a living being" (Gen. 1:27; 2:7 *New Life Version*).

This awesome Being who revealed himself to be God made each one of us. Mind-boggling, I know. It is incredible to think about the fact that the one who spoke solar systems into orbit and who holds the universe together by his power, chose to create you and me, uniquely.

But why?

Why did he create us? The Bible is very clear on this point. Every person throughout history was created for the sole purpose of bringing glory to our Creator. Yes, girls, we were created to shine! In Isaiah 43:6–7, the Lord said, "Bring my sons from afar and my daughters from the ends of the earth—everyone who is called by my name, whom I created for my glory" (NIV).

Did you notice the last part of that verse? God says we were created for *his* glory, not our own. We are designed to make *his* name known, to lift high *his* praise, to turn the spotlight on *his* face.

Like stars that light up the night sky, we are designed to shine—to reflect to the world that our God is incredibly glorious. Author and speaker John Piper in his book *Don't Waste Your Life* explains this purpose: "God created me—and you—to live with a single, all-embracing, all-transforming passion—namely, a passion to glorify God by enjoying and displaying his supreme excellence in all the spheres of life."[2]

We are created to make God's glory known, yet we live in and struggle against a culture that claims *we (the created ones)* are the center of the universe—not God (the Creator). Shining for God's glory is a radical shift from the cry of the world that says, "Make much of yourself!" Our education, marketing, and, sadly, even our parents have spent years programming us to believe that we (the individual) are the most important person on earth. Self-esteem is the highest virtue. Love of self is the utmost concern. It is not only common but expected for people to place their needs and priorities above all else.

> **We are created to make God's glory known, yet we live in and struggle against a culture that claims we are the center of the universe—not God.**

Honestly, we all can fall prey to purpose-shifting philosophies. I hear people all the time say, "I just want to be happy." As well as the politically correct version of this statement, "whatever makes someone happy." Here's the big problem with that statement. Happiness is not the purpose of life. The purpose of life is "to glorify God and enjoy Him forever."[3] And, we will never know real and lasting "happiness" if we are not doing what we were created to do. To seek our personal happiness as the chief objective of life is to go against our created design.[4]

Purpose

This begs the question: can we truly be "happy" or feel "content" if we aren't doing the very thing we were created to do in the first place? I would argue that it's absolutely impossible. This is the fish-out-of-water syndrome. Pursuing our own fame and glory turns the purpose of life upside down and ultimately leaves us completely empty and questioning what life is really all about.

Rick Warren in his best-selling book *The Purpose Driven Life* hit the nail on the head with his opening sentence, "It's not about you." Ouch! But as tough as that is to hear,

> Pursuing our own fame and glory turns the purpose of life upside down and ultimately leaves us completely empty and questioning what life is really all about.

I love his straight-shooting and matter-of-fact approach. He doesn't break the news to us gently. Instead, Warren confronts our celebrity-seeking, me-first generation with the hard truth—life is not about us. To know the purpose of life, we must begin with God and with the purpose for which he created us—to bring him glory.

What does it mean to glorify God?

To glorify means "to reflect, show forth, demonstrate and express the image of an object or person so that it may be seen by all." Therefore, glorifying *God* is acting like a mirror—reflecting

SHINE

his presence, *his* essence, *his* life, and *his* name. To boil all of this down to a single statement: Glorifying God simply means making much of *him,* to make *him* famous (John 14:13; 16:14; 17:1, 5). So, what does all of this theology have to do with the List?

I'm so very glad you asked.

Consumed

I spent many empty years pursuing my List, believing the lie that if I could just attain all the little check marks, then I would be fulfilled. Here's the truth: There is never enough. There is always just a little more to be accomplished, achieved, or acquired. The dogma of our time tells us that through consuming we will find happiness: consuming relationships, consuming possessions, and, ultimately, consuming glory for ourselves. Ironically, *the* secret to life is not found in consuming but in being consumed—consumed by a passion for God and his glory that overflows our lives like a mighty rushing river.

Before I became a follower of Jesus Christ, I, too, was that girl clamoring for center stage. I needed, *desperately* needed, to be up front, onstage, and made much of. The reason? I did not know my purpose. My soul didn't know the reason for my existence; therefore, I bought into the lie the world sells, which says happiness is found in making much of Marian. And I was miserable. Miserable, that is, until I met Jesus.

> The secret to life is not found in consuming but in being consumed—consumed by a passion for God.

21

But first, back to my agony.

Here's the thing, in a family of seven siblings you are never the star for long. Oh, don't get me wrong, I tried. But it seemed no matter what kind of drama I could create and diversions I could cause, I couldn't stay center stage when competing with home-run hitters, beautiful sisters, and endless bouts with broken bones and chicken pox.

Want the real truth? I was born into a family of five older siblings. There I was, the BABY. I was "practically perfect in every way," complete with curly blonde hair and a big toothless grin. Yes, adorable and adored. And then—pause here for effect—my baby brother was born . . . with no right hand *and* half-blind! Talk about a scene stealer! The audacity of some people . . . he had to go and ruin my life! Seriously, how completely self-centered could he be to come into this world with such distractions? And so, faster than you could say "special needs," my status in the family dynamic was quickly usurped.

If you think this sounds harsh, you are correct. You see, the Enemy places a hard edge around our hearts. So much so, that sometimes we don't even realize we are hard-hearted in our pursuit of attention and adoration. Oh, my brother and I are very close now, and our family history is fraught with hilarious tales of rivalry. Today, we are both followers of Jesus and know life works best when we give him center stage.

You see, Jesus is the fullness of God's glory, the only one who deserves exaltation, and it is he who teaches us the way to *real* life. The Bible says concerning him:

The Word [Jesus] became flesh and took up residence among us. We observed His glory, the glory as the One and Only Son from the Father, full of grace and truth. (John 1:14)

He [Jesus] is the radiance of His glory, the exact expression of His nature, and He sustains all things by His powerful word. (Heb. 1:3)

Let's break this one down a bit, shall we? In following Jesus, we behold God's glory in him. In turn, we reflect his glory to the world (i.e., we fulfill our purpose). You see, this is what our culture doesn't understand: We *are* designed to shine—not unto ourselves, but as reflections of the glorious One. Just as the moon reflects the light of the sun, we, too, are designed to reflect Jesus, the Light of the world. And here's the beautiful bonus: When we do what we were created to do, we discover joy—the pure joy that comes only from living out our ultimate purpose.

When I surrendered my life to Jesus Christ, a passion for God's glory consumed me. Not only did he forgive my sin (miracle of all miracles), but he showed me a new way to live—for the glory of his name in any and every situation. As I studied the Bible and saw God more clearly—exalted in his majesty, magnificent in his beauty, and his glory as the all-consuming reason for living— a fiery love for his fame gripped my heart. It was at this point that I remember worshipping the Lord and thinking to myself,

> **Just as the moon reflects the light of the sun, we, too, are designed to reflect Jesus, the Light of the world.**

I'm alive, I'm alive, I'm alive . . . I'm alive! In doing the very thing God created me to do, exalting him, I felt life as it was meant to be experienced for the first time.

Little did I know at that time what an intense battle rages over glory.

The War for Center Stage

Since the dawn of time, a battle has raged over the coveted spot of center stage; this is the war for glory. This cosmic conflict is fought by Satan, God's adversary and the enemy of humanity, and the Creator himself. The Bible teaches us that Satan was originally the most beautiful of God's creatures in heaven. He was the chief angel, whose specific purpose was to reflect the light of God's glory, but evil entered his heart and he craved this brilliance for himself. Because of his desire to be the famous one, Satan (at that time called Lucifer, the morning star) was cast out of heaven, taking one-third of the angelic host with him (Rev. 12:1–12; Ezek. 28:11–19; Isa. 14:12–17).

This is where you and I enter the scene. When God created the world, he established it in perfection. He placed Adam and Eve in the Garden of Eden and gave them dominion and purpose (Gen. 1–2). It was there, in the garden, that Satan attacked God's glory by tempting Eve into sin (Gen. 3:1–4). He deceived her into believing happiness could be found by seeking her own glory, instead of the glory of her Creator. He promised her power, prestige, and position—to be *somebody* who is made much of (v. 5). Eve took the bait and so did Adam, resulting in all of humanity falling from glory.

Today, we battle the same Enemy and face the same choice in every temptation—glorify self or glorify God? All sin comes down to this one question. In seeking our own glory we find emptiness, destruction, and death simply because we are choosing to turn the purpose of life upside down.

But God . . .

One of my all-time favorite faith phrases is "but God." In my mind, this little ditty is translated: Despite how bad things may look, there is still hope because God is always in the equation. Check this out: the Bible says, *"But God* demonstrates his own love for us in this: While we were *still sinners,* Christ died for us" (Rom. 5:8 NIV, emphasis mine). That is the amazing thing about God. While we were still grasping after his glory, he chose to die for us, setting us free from the death and destruction that comes from our devastating decisions.

> Today, we battle the same Enemy and face the same choice in every temptation— glorify self or glorify God?

I'm so excited to tell you the next part that I can hardly sit still. The speaker/teacher/preacher/evangelist in me wants to stand before you, wave my arms, jump up and down, and exclaim with as much passion as my soul can muster: "IT IS IN THE DEATH AND RESURRECTION OF JESUS CHRIST THAT THE ULTIMATE WAR FOR GOD'S GLORY IS WON! YES, WON!" By dying on the cross, Jesus Christ glorified the grace, mercy, kindness, justice, holiness, goodness, faithfulness, and love of his heavenly Father in rescuing you and me from sin. The sacrificial death of Jesus testifies to the world, in capital letters, GOD IS GLORIOUS!

Please tell me you comprehend the enormousness of that statement. This is huge. Massive, really. Don't make me show up at each one of your doorsteps and give you a personal shoulder-shaking explanation of how incredible this is.

I simply don't have that many frequent flyer miles.

Girls, the glory of God is the reason Jesus died for you and for me. Satan, the liar, deceiver, and glory robber is defeated at the cross of Christ. OK, it's time for you to get a little crazy with me girls. Shout hallelujah! Do a little dance and get your praise on with me!

Whew! I feel better.

Oh, but I forgot, there's just one more thing. Even though Satan *is* ultimately defeated, he doesn't stop *trying* to destroy God's glory in our lives every single day. His MO (mode of operation) is the same. He comes to steal, kill, and destroy, and his preferred methodology is still deception (John 10:10); therefore, we must be on guard. Our Enemy knows that he can never take our salvation, 100 percent secured by the finished work of Christ; Satan can, however, tempt us away from our ultimate purpose (glorifying God through our attitudes and actions) and, in doing so, make our lives incredibly miserable. I've heard it said many times, "Satan can never steal our salvation, but he will try every single day to steal our testimony."

The Power of a Testimony

As an author and speaker, I travel often with my work. For this reason, I'm blessed to see and experience the uniqueness of this amazing country of ours. Just recently, I happened upon another cultural phenom . . . the fried pie. Now, if you are from the South, you've probably experienced the delicious goodness I'm about to describe. If not, then I'm sorry for so many reasons.

- The fried pie is exactly what the name implies—a pie that is fried.
- Within the flaky, folded fried dough, one can put her choice of filling: peach, blueberry, chocolate, pecan, and, of course, apple.

I'm an apple girl.

I encountered this carb and sugar gold mine off Route 77 in Oklahoma just three miles shy of the high road to Falls Creek Camp. But, girls, let me just say my mouth started watering the minute I saw the gigantic billboard on the interstate promising Fried Pies Ahead, miles before I arrived. When I saw the sign, I began explaining to my traveling companions my affinity for the fried pie. You see, my grandmother made these for me when I was a little girl, *and* you can get all the goodness of an apple pie in a convenient hand-size package.

I'm just sayin' . . . What's not to love?

As we neared the exit, I thought to myself, "Will my skinny little girlfriends really want to stop for a treat?" Then, clearing my throat, I asked, "Do you think we have enough time for a quick detour?" From the backseat my size 0 friend said, "Girl, you had me at fried pie."

You simply have no idea how much I loved all ninety-five pounds of her in that moment.

Elated with our off-the-beaten-path discovery, we veered off our route for what I like to call fried pie paradise. Once inside, we walked straight up to the counter where we were greeted by the loveliest woman you'll ever meet. I'm sure it's hard not to be bubbly when you're making other people so incredibly happy all day long.

I digress.

After much debate amongst my traveling crew concerning apple or apricot and to split or not to split—we finally landed on two pies each, in a variety of flavors, so that we could each get a nibble.

My words fail. Grandma, I'm sorry, but that was the best thing I've ever tasted.

So, like I said, I was in Oklahoma that particular weekend to speak at a women's conference. Naturally, before I began my first talk, I described *in detail* and with *much* passion the fried pie experience.

I praised the assorted fruit fillings.

I explained extensively how each pie is lovingly constructed *and deep-fried* before your eyes.

I extolled the excellent virtues and convenience of a hand-held dessert.

Let's just say I brought much glory to the fried pie industry in my five-minute spiel. Fast-forward two days.

On our way back to the airport, we decided we must stop again at fried pie paradise and stock up for the flight home. Pulling back in the parking lot, we gasped at the sight before our eyes. There was now a line wrapping through the building and out into the parking lot! It seems my testimony had power.

As I stood in line (for nearly an hour, I might add) to purchase my road trip treat, I thought about the power of a testimony. A testimony is simply one person's account of something. As Christians, our testimonies are our explanation of who God is and what he has done in our lives so that others will be drawn to him and desire to know him as we do. I hoped and prayed that day that the women from the conference walked away with far more than a tip on a great place to get dessert. My greatest desire is that they know my Redeemer. That experience taught me a powerful lesson: If women would testify about Jesus with the same amount of passion and enthusiasm we do about new shoes, new recipes, new sales, new diet secrets, then our testimonies would rock this world with God's grace.

> **As Christians, our testimonies are our explanation of who God is and what he has done in our lives so that others will be drawn to him and desire to know him as we do.**

I can't help but think about how this truth applies to the seasons when we are waiting for God to fulfill the dreams found on our list. So often in this season of waiting for God to provide, we live in a spirit of complaining and despair. When we choose to live this way, Satan robs us of our joy, and, as a result, we cease to glorify God with our attitude and words. Looking back, my biggest regret from my single years is the time wasted allowing Satan to make me feel miserable.

You see, my friends, flat-out miserable is exactly how I felt in the months leading up to that big-fat-horrible birthday I tried so hard to avoid. Now I know why. Somewhere along the way I was deceived. Although I was head over heels in love with Jesus and longed to glorify him in every area of my life, I fell for the lie that God wasn't good and my life was incomplete because I had yet to complete the goals on *my* List. My focus shifted from exalting God to exalting my desires. I listened to Satan, the father of lies, and allowed seeds of discontentment to bud in my heart.

Here's the thing: Satan knows that joy is a testimony to the glory of God—it makes Jesus irresistible to others. Joy overflows from a heart that believes God's promises are true and knows he is faithfully working all circumstances in life for good. Contentment and peace attract others to Jesus because those blessings are impossible apart from him; therefore, Satan aims his arrows at our hearts seeking to destroy our joy and diminish God's glory in us. He whispers . . .

> "God has blessings in store for everyone but you."
> "The promises in the Bible are just a big lie."
> "The desires of your heart will never be met if you
>   trust God."

Guess how I responded to his lies? I can tell you one thing: my attitude sure wasn't glorifying to God. Joy, the hallmark of the Christian faith, was noticeably MIA, and my words certainly weren't praising God for my circumstances. Sadly, for a season, I believed Satan's accusations about God's goodness, and I acted like a spoiled little brat. OK, perhaps that is a little harsh self-assessment. No, I didn't storm about throwing a tantrum, but I did temporarily forget the amazing blessings I had and doubted his plan for my life.

Killing Bridezilla

I learned an important lesson through that experience: Satan loves turning our circumstances into opportunities for whining sessions—full-throttle fits that would make even the best Bridezilla cringe. When we fall for the temptation to whine and complain, it affects our emotional state of being, and we become miserable women. But when we choose to believe the truth that God is good and that he delights in blessing his children, we can surrender our Lists (the unmet longings and desires of our hearts), trusting that his plan and his timing are *far* better than our own.

> When we fall for the temptation to whine and complain, it affects our emotional state of being, and we become miserable women.

As cheesy as this may sound, I KNOW Garth Brooks is right when he sings, "Thank God for unanswered prayers!" Reflecting on that season, I can honestly say that back then my chief desire was far more about *my* glory than I would have probably admitted; it was my desire to be married. Actually, I'm not even sure I wanted to be married as much as I wanted to be a bride. I longed for my own here-comes-the-bride-all-dressed-in-white moment. I think a little Bridezilla was lurking inside of me that desperately wanted center stage . . . *and* the perfect place setting, of course.

I CANNOT BELIEVE I JUST CONFESSED THAT!

I'm 1,000 percent certain that my perception of marriage (at that time) wasn't really about making a lifelong covenant with a flawed and imperfect person (by the way girls, they all are) 'til death do us part. Nope, back then, getting married was all about the wedding: the ring, the dress, the flowers, the reception, and shining as queen for the ~~day, week~~ . . . Who am I kidding? I just wanted to be the queen.

Demanding center stage in life is the quickest route to misery.

I'm so thankful the Lord spared me and some poor chap years of misery. Marriage is impossible when one or both people are trying to be number one. I'm forever grateful that God didn't fulfill my List on my timetable, allowing me the dream wedding that would have ended up being a total nightmare.

Thankfully the Lord revealed to me my biggest problem. I had lost sight of my true purpose. My List was all about making much of Marian. The Lord showed me that I was pursuing my own glory, and this was the real cause of my despair. This, my friend, is the big glitch with a Bridezillatude.

Demanding center stage in life is the quickest route to misery.

When a girl is focused on her own glory at the expense of others, she will never be happy. For starters, nothing is ever good enough, people never do enough, and try as one may, the rest of the world simply fails to get the memo that life is all about making much of her. Therefore, she ends up feeling frustrated, jealous, hurt, and angry when she gives into the temptation to make life all about her.

> By teaching me to center my life on his glory, God rescued me from the horrible pit of self-pity that comes from being a Bridezilla.

The reason self-glorification makes us miserable is because it is the opposite of our designed purpose. And if this problem is not addressed, it can, and will, cause us misery in every season of life—school life, single life, married life, mommy life, career life. Essentially, you could acquire your List and become one miserable woman *if* your List is all about you.

The Sweet Spot

Here's the bottom line: when God reminded me of my true purpose, which is the number one goal on his List, he saved me from myself. By teaching me to center my life on his glory, God rescued me from the horrible pit of self-pity that comes from being a Bridezilla—the seemingly paradoxical combination of self-glorification and self-loathing that only our me-first culture could create.

Girls, in renewing my true purpose God freed me to shine, *really* shine. Living with the spotlight on the face of Jesus is the only way to live. I was made to make much of him!

I like to call *this* place the sweet spot.

For those of you unfamiliar with baseball, the sweet spot is where the ball and bat connect at the perfect place, and wham! Home run! My oldest brother, Matt, is an incredible athlete and baseball was his game. Some of my earliest childhood memories are of cheering for him on hot summer nights. Popcorn. Snow cones. Mosquitoes buzzing. Fans cheering. The crackle of an old PA system.

I'll never forget hearing the crack of his bat when it connected with the ball on the sweet spot. We all knew where to look, because that sucker was flying over the left-field fence.

Home run! The crowd goes wild!

Girls, this is how life feels when we center our lives on God's glory. When we connect with his purpose, the result is glorious! Now, after a miserable season of seeking a different kind of glory, my words fail to tell you how good it is to be back.

My soul is filled.

My joy is overflowing.

My heart is at rest.

Life is simply brilliant in the sweet spot!

> *Wherever you are, be all there.*
> *Live to the hilt every situation you*
> *believe to be the will of God.*
>
> —Jim Elliot

Hope

To make your season beautiful, become a girl who flat out believes God.

*You know how when you were a little kid and you believed in
fairy tales, that fantasy of what your life would be, white dress,
prince charming who would carry you away to a castle on a hill.
You would lie in bed at night and close your eyes and you had
complete and utter faith. Santa Claus, the Tooth Fairy, Prince
Charming, they were so close you could taste them, but eventually you
grow up, one day you open your eyes and the fairy tale disappears. . . .
But the thing is, it's hard to let go of that fairy tale entirely 'cause
almost everyone has that smallest bit of hope, of faith, that one
day they will open their eyes and it will come true.*
—MEREDITH GREY, *GREY'S ANATOMY*

Can You Keep a Secret?

I have an addiction.

It is quite embarrassing actually. Please promise me you won't judge. It takes a huge amount of trust for me to open up and confess this secret to you. OK, so here I go, "Hello, my name is Marian, and I am absolutely addicted to infomercials." There. I said it. Some of you may be asking, *what* is an infomercial? Oooooh, let me explain. An infomercial is a half-hour-long commercial that hocks everything from body-sculpting workouts to age-reversal eye creams. Yes, for a reason to be named later, watching those wretchedly annoying things is my new warped fixation.

Like I said, so very embarrassing.

Here's how I usually get my fix. Flipping through the nine hundred channels, looking for something completely mind stimulating like *American Idol* or *Lost*, I happen upon a paid-for-product placement, otherwise known as the infomercial. Like a fly into a high-speeding windshield, I am sucked into these commercials with such impressive velocity that I often find myself fixated, remote still pointed at the TV, and unmoved for several minutes.

The promises are always so very believable.

In those captivating moments, I've watched hordes of promises from cellulite banishers, miraculous wrinkle reducers, plastic food-storage containers, hair-straightening irons, and, of course, a plethora of exercise machines. The promises are always so very believable. Viewers like me are persuaded with the real-life testimonials, the amazing before-and-after photos, fancy digitalized dramatizations, and, most important, the celebrity endorsements. Who in their right mind wouldn't believe these promises that buying the product wouldn't absolutely change her life?

One of my new favorites to watch is a commercial for a product line called Meaningful Beauty. This product promises to give you *and me* flawless skin free of all those hideous signs of aging—blotchiness, under-eye circles, and the not-so-funny laugh lines. In order to validate the claims of the product, the spokeswoman is none other than Cindy Crawford, the girl who put the *super* in supermodel. Who wouldn't trust super-Cindy? In addition, potential buyers get the expertise of a world-renowned French dermatologist. After all, everyone knows the French know *everything* about creating beautiful skin. At this point I'm hooked. These guys are simply brilliant because within minutes I am completely convinced that the product that has left Cindy Crawford both beautiful and breathtaking will do the very same for me. And should a little doubt still remain, there is a 100 percent money-back guarantee. Of course there is.

We adore a money-back guarantee, don't we? The pledge to doubting consumers that says, "Trust me, everything is going to be just fine." So, with that added measure of security, we buy, trusting that the claims and promises of the product are true.

Want to know the *real* secret to a great infomercial? Lean in a little closer because this one is just between us—the secret to an infomercial is *what* it is selling. No, I'm not referring to the product, silly. The secret is in *what* the product promises. The infomercial promises us something that we would gladly pay the required $29.99 for the rest of our lives to possess. So what is it the advertisers are *really* selling? If you pay close attention, you will quickly recognize that these clever marketers aren't promoting exercise machines or skin cream. Nope, my friend, they are hocking hope.

Hocking Hope

For every woman, beginning to see the telltale signs of aging and fearing the consequences of her crow's feet, the new miracle skin-care line is *hope* for a younger and more desirable-looking future. For the young adult who suffers emotionally and socially from acne, the clear-skin product is *hope* for a blemish and rejection-free future. For the overweight mom who feels invisible and unattractive, then the latest and greatest home gym equipment is *hope* for a slimmer and more attractive physique in the future.

Hope sells.

Hope is the reason we scramble to find our credit cards, grab the phone, and dial that 800 number. There's just something inside of us that hopes, call it an *intangible* feeling, that all of those promises made on television may actually quiet the cry of our soul's deeper and truer desires. You know, those secret longings often unexpressed but tapped into by marketing geniuses. Temporarily, the product becomes the object of our hope—the thing we *believe* will improve our circumstances, give us completion, or change our reality . . . for the better.

Girls, it is all about hope.

Hope is the most powerful tool to lift the human spirit. Marketers know it is the key ingredient required in selling. Hope sells because it is the very emotion that buoys us in the sea of life. Simply offer people the expectation of a better, brighter, and more beautiful future, and . . . cha-ching!

As I write these words, I wrestle with the ability to answer the question: What is hope? The word has so many different connotations that I know I must clarify the meaning. *Hope* is defined as "a feeling of expectation and desire."[1] I define *hope* as desire with the expectation of fulfillment. The word *expectation* is so huge, for expecting is the activity of hope. When I hope, I choose to place my expectation in the thing I believe will deliver a good and positive outcome.

A great illustration of this concept was drawn for me while touring New York City. When taking a cruise around Manhattan, our guide casually mentioned some notable facts about Ellis Island—the first stop for immigrants entering the United States from destinations around the world. Most came to America escaping persecution or political and economic instability. For those worn and weary travelers, coming to America was a journey of hope.

There, on Ellis Island immigrants learned their fate. In the Great Hall each immigrant awaited the government's decision. Acceptance or denial? On hearing their fate, they would exit either through the Hall of Tears or the Hall of Hope. The latter meant a future in America.

I can just imagine an Irish family in the early 1900s, fleeing the famine that killed thousands in their homeland, walking that hallway into the bright sunshine of a new life. Rightly named, for many this was a walk of hope. They believed, trusted, expected, and, yes, hoped that life would be better for them in America.

A Bad Case of the BLD!

Thinking back to my List, I see now that it was composed of the things I believed would provide joy, happiness, and security in this life I'm livin'. You know, like meeting a great guy, landing the perfect job, earning a huge income, attaining a beautiful appearance, and acquiring the right stuff (the newest gadget, the latest handbag—whatever my favorite fashion magazine told me I "must have" in order to have my best life now).

My hope was in my List.

Education + Travel + Mr. Right + 2-carat diamond
+ 2.5 kids + 4-bedroom home = Happy Marian

Here's what I know *now* that I didn't know then. Whenever hope is misplaced, disappointment soon follows. I like to call this the Big Letdown, or simply, the BLD between us friends. There is not a girl on planet Earth who has not experienced the BLD at some point in her life.

> **Whenever hope is misplaced, disappointment soon follows.**

This may sound silly to some of you, but consider the girl who thought she would *d-i-e* if she did not make cheerleader in high school. Seriously, I know it may sound trite, but she could not face the possibility that she would not be wearing "the uniform" on game days. Number one on her List was CHEERLEADER, in all capital letters. She had been dreaming, practicing, and jumping for this day since she could walk. Put yourself in her Nikes for a minute. Cheerleading was her childhood dream. She'd even taken "lessons" from the big girls in her neighborhood. So, on that day in high school, after an extremely well-executed toe-touch, tryouts were over and the waiting began. When her name was finally called, life was . . . well, perfect. Complete. That is, until the drudgery of after-school practices and competitive girl cattiness set in. Then, to her surprise, cheerleading quickly became a drag and certainly not the ideal life she always imagined.

Her hopes now turned to homecoming, (ahem) becoming the homecoming QUEEN, that is. Cheerleading was now NBD (no big deal). It was the crown that really mattered. She'd moved on to the next item on her List. But this time, as she sat in history class, anxiously listening as the homecoming court was announced, she experienced another BLD. For when *that* List is finished, hers remains unchecked.

The disappointment is crushing . . . for you see this is bigger than just homecoming. Her *hope* for acceptance and approval (which becoming Queen symbolized) was wrapped tightly in that crown.

Meet Claire

Claire was a beautiful and flourishing thirty-two-year-old executive living in the heart of New York City. Her childhood dream as the younger sister of two highly successful brothers was to one day be the very best in her field and earn the respect of her male coworkers . . . not to mention her family. Claire was both driven and determined. She worked extremely hard to climb the corporate ladder. Each promotion gave her a momentary sense of satisfaction, but the pleasure success brought was short-lived, and her joy faded as quickly as she eyed the career rungs still ahead of her. Claire would not be satisfied until she reached the top. Ironically, Claire's BLD occurred when she *attained* her List.

I remember thinking to myself, "Finally I've arrived!" This is the life I've hoped for since I was a little girl. Unlike most women, my List never consisted of meeting Prince Charming or any other of those fairy-tale stories. No, I dreamed of being an independent, successful, and wealthy career woman. My List was filled with power and possessions.

I'll never forget my big letdown. I was finally promoted to vice president (the only female VP in my company, to be precise). To celebrate, I treated myself to a luxurious vacation in the south of France. In my mind, this glamorous getaway was the perfect reward—a beautiful villa, fine food, and a fast European convertible. Only the best, or so I thought.

42

Sitting in my extremely expensive business-class seat on a trans-Atlantic flight from New York to Paris, I was aware of the old familiar feeling of dissatisfaction. My seat, which once seemed so superior to economy class, felt poor and pathetic in comparison to the first-class seat I now longed for just a few feet away. As I sat there, despairing my misfortune, it occurred to me that my two-bedroom flat in London (provided by my company), which at first felt glamorous and spacious, now seemed like a college dorm room with cramped closets and no room for my ever-growing shoe collection.

When I arrived in France and cast my eyes on the silver-spooned ladies of St. Tropez, the red Peugeot convertible that transported me from the airport to a villa in the vineyards now felt like a donkey taking me to a broken-down farmhouse. Clothed in diamonds and designers, these women owned mansions, and their limo drivers whisked them away from the airport before I could even manage to get my keys from the rental car company.

That week, I realized there would never, ever be enough of anything. Ironically, in the lap of luxury, I discovered it was impossible for my List to bring me happiness. Instead, I felt exhausted, overspent, and disappointed. Exhausted from busting my tail to beat the boys for position after position only to "arrive," and still not feel satisfied, overspent because there was always some new label that was the "must have" of the moment, and disappointed because I realized that no matter how big the house, how fast the car, or how many pairs of Jimmy Choo's I was able to acquire, I still was not happy.

Both of these young women have one thing in common: Their hope was placed in their List, and, in the end, they felt bitterly disappointed.

New Year's Eve

I've never been a big fan of New Year's Eve. Even back in my wild, BC (*before Christ*) days, it was the one event that always fell flat, disappointing. It reeked BLD. Yet, for many years, like millions around the globe, I got all dolled up to celebrate.

You want to know why? *Hope.* Sure, I'll admit it. I fell for the hype. The lofty expectation that something spectacular would occur . . . something akin to *When Harry Met Sally* . . . or *Sleepless in Seattle* (the entire New Year's Eve industry owes a debt of gratitude to Meg Ryan). Many years I believed the buzz from friends who said, "Woo-hoo, it's going to be the best night of the year. We will have sooooooo much fun." So, against my better judgment, I'd forgo my true desire to watch a Jane Austen movie marathon, while eating takeout *and* clothed in flannel, and I'd give in to the voices crying out to me to make plans for the "best night of the year." You may call me Debbie Downer, but if we're being honest, I'd much rather be at home in my pjs, curled up watching *Pride and Prejudice* (the five-hour, BBC, Colin Firth version, of course).

Needless to say, you will never find me amongst the masses ringing in New Year's at the most famous location of all—New York City. Every year, as the clock nears midnight, the eyes of the world turn to the dazzling lights and bustling energy of Times Square. Anticipation runs high. New Year's Eve in the heart of New York City has become more than just a celebration—it's a global tradition. The world holds its breath and cheers as the clock strikes twelve. As the famous ball descends, over a billion viewers throughout the world unite in bidding a collective farewell to the departing year and expressing their joy and *hope* for the year ahead.

In his memoir *Dispatches from the Edge*, journalist Anderson Cooper reflects on covering the Times Square New Year's Eve celebration and the hope felt on this night.

> When midnight arrives, the air explodes into a solid mass, a swirl of colored confetti that seems to hang suspended in space . . . the air seems to shake, and for a few brief moments I feel part of something larger, not lost in the crowd, but swept up by it, buoyed by the emotion, the energy, the joyful pandemonium. It overwhelms my defenses, my hard-won cynicism. The past gives way to the present, and I give myself up to it—the possibilities, the potential.[2]

"Swept up." I love how Anderson describes this moment. The emotional feeling of hope lifts us out of the present—through the power of imagination—projects us to where the fulfillment of our desires dwell. Hope is a wish, a dream, a longing. The possibilities fill us with joy. Elation. Jubilation. Euphoria. Hope can be an incredible feeling, but *real* hope is so much more than a feeling.

So often, after an emotional high like Cooper describes, we awake on New Year's Day let down from the cloud. Like our ill-fated resolutions, the emotional high of hope conjured up with the confetti doesn't last. We count down the past, expecting change in our future. Then when we wake up on January 1, the same people with the same problems, we are often disappointed. Reality sets in. The euphoria, in a swirl of confetti and midnight kisses, was just a fleeting emotional experience—not anything of *real* substance—just wishful thinking. Most of the time "wishful thinking" is what most people mean when they say, "I hope." What they mean is, "I wish."

No certainty.

No security.

No confidence.

The Bible has a different definition of hope—a confident expectation. Confidence that is rooted in faith—that the object of our hope is trustworthy, dependable, and reliable.

False Hope

The big letdowns in life happen when we place our hope in the wrong thing. Real hope is so much more than a feeling. In order for hope to be true and lasting, it must be placed in something sure and solid. Biblical hope—greater than unsteady emotions—proves an anchor for the soul.

Psalm 33 explains the difference between false and real hope. The psalmist began by praising God for his incredible attributes: power, strength, sovereignty, wisdom, love, and faithfulness. He then reminded us that God is intimately aware and acquainted with our deepest needs and desires, for our hearts were fashioned uniquely *by* him. He knows us. He formed us. He spoke the world into existence and sustains it by his power. In other words, the first fifteen verses lay the foundation for why the Lord is the only one worthy of our hope. Then, in verse 16, our attention turns to the "false hopes" in which we are so quick to put our trust.

> The king is not saved by a mighty army; A warrior is not delivered by great strength. A horse is a *false hope* for victory; nor does it deliver anyone by its great strength. (NASB, emphasis mine)

This psalm was written to remind God's people that there is only one source of security . . . and it's not their military prowess. There is only one source of deliverance . . . and it is not in human power. Trusting, relying, and depending on anything created—instead of our Creator—is illustrating a false hope.

One of my favorite things about God is his absolute sureness in himself. Frankly, God does not suffer with self-esteem issues. He *knows* he is the all-powerful, all-knowing, sovereign Lord. He loves when his children hope in him because they, too, believe he is who he says he is. This is where hope and faith go hand in hand.

We hope in the object of our faith. We hope in what we believe will deliver.

Psalm 33 was written because God's people are so quick to trust in false hopes. Take the nation of Israel for example. The Lord rescued the Israelites from Egyptian slavery by defeating Pharaoh and his armies. Then God supernaturally led them with a cloud by day and pillar of fire by night. (Girls, can you just imagine a "pillar of fire"? Hello?) Meanwhile, they beheld his miraculous powers (such as providing bread from heaven, water from rocks, parting seas . . . just your everyday God stuff). Last but not least, he amazed them by repeatedly defeating their enemies.

Yes, for those of you keeping score at home, these are the same people who later turned away from their Redeemer and put their hope for deliverance in something special like a golden cow, or on really special occasions, little wooden idols they carved themselves. And we all know how that worked out for them. NOT SO GOOD. Their idolatry always led to bondage and destruction. Yet, each time God mercifully rescued them from the devastation that was the result of trusting in something false.

This psalm was also written to you and me because we are exactly like Israel, easily swayed into relying on something bogus. OK. So not many people these days are bowing down to golden calves, but we are quick to hope in money, material possessions, or a man for our security.

In the original language of the Bible, the word used here for "false hope" also translates as a lie, a sham, or a deception.

Girlfriends, I liken this to the anticellulite creams I see advertised. I'm just sayin' (and I beg forgiveness from cosmetic companies globally), we all know the stuff doesn't work. It's a big fat lie (no pun intended). But seriously, no amount of lotion applied in a circular motion is going to banish years of key lime pie. I'm just sayin' big fat, false hope, and big fat thighs.

Quick definition. A false hope is relying on or trusting in something other than God for life, security, deliverance, power, or protection. The lies are false because they aren't reliable; they can *and* will let us down, and ultimately, they are not *worthy* of our trust. Essentially this psalm warns that we must be extremely careful that we aren't swindled, suckered, or conned into placing our hope in a fraud.

> **A false hope is relying on or trusting in something other than God for life, security, deliverance, power, or protection.**

Let's look at verses 16–17 from a girl's perspective, shall we? After all, the last time I checked, not too many girls I know place their trust in armies, warriors, or horses, but the principle is the same for us.

- The princess is not rescued by her knight in shining armor.
- A woman is not delivered by her great beauty.
- Money is a false hope for security.
- Neither boys, beauty, or handbags deliver fulfillment.

I'm the first to admit I've believed the lie of false hopes. What girl hasn't? We are bombarded with messages that beg us to trust in or depend on anything other than God for our security. Our favorite chick flicks feed the notion that in meeting Mr. Right we will find our Hollywood happy ending. Our favorite magazines tell us to trust in our beauty and bodies to earn love . . . or at least some momentary attention. Or better yet, feminism encourages us to become a self-reliant, independent, I-don't-need-anyone tough girl who hopes only in herself for her future.

Here's the problem: There is only one God. Only one firm foundation. There is only one who is 100 percent reliable, trustworthy, dependable, and capable of knowing and meeting our every need. Trusting in false hopes is like stepping onto a surface that you believe is solid only to discover you're in sinking sand.

Sinking Sand to Solid Ground

I longed for something solid. Firm ground on which to stand. Yet, my life before Jesus felt like a ship tossed about on a stormy sea. My emotions, vacillating from giddy to grave, lurched up and down with the rise of hopeful expectations and the fall of crushing letdowns. Each day was a date with uncertainty. Would today be good or bad? Would I feel happy or sad? Would I be up or down? The answer depended on the object of my hope—my job, my friends, my looks, my crush, my grades, my weight, my popularity, my achievements, my plans for the weekend. I did not know the meaning of *real* hope before I began a relationship with God through Jesus.

Rewind. I must tell you a little of my history. From childhood through college, I was not a girl who hoped in God. Sure, I knew information *about* God. Growing up in a small Texas town, church attendance was an expected tradition. It seemed everyone I knew went on Sunday. Christianity was just facts, not my faith. I knew about Jesus, I just didn't *know* Jesus. I sang the hymns, heard the stories, and could even quote a few Bible verses, but my hope for happiness, life, security, and completion was in everything the world had to offer.

As far back as I can recall, I fell for the facade of false hopes— the gilded promises seemed so believable. I remember going to middle school with the number one goal of "becoming popular." I thought, *If I'm popular then I will feel accepted.* Therefore, I was constantly conforming myself to the crowd and hoping for the approval of my peers to make me feel like I belonged. As a late teen, I believed the wild party scene would bring me happiness. I began binge drinking in pursuit of the intoxicating high I hoped would provide me escape. As I grew older, I bought the lie that sex outside of marriage was "no big deal," and would make me feel treasured. I gave myself away in hope that I would find the love I craved. Entering adulthood, I trusted in the promises of marketing companies that if I purchased their products, my life would be complete, so I charged up the credit cards, hoping the next shopping spree would rid me of my emptiness.

The result? Big letdowns followed by even *bigger* letdowns. I was a girl overspent, overworked, overused, and over-her-head in disappointment from chasing her List. In the midst of one especially emotional storm, I cried out to God. Nothing spectacular or poetic, just a simple prayer, *Help.*

A few weeks later a friend invited me to visit her church. Sure, I'd done the church thing as a kid, but this time it was different. Chalk it up to desperation or just great timing, but for the first time in my life, as I listened to the message, something clicked.

Not rules.

Not religion.

Just Jesus.

I realized the gospel is a message of hope: God became a man, entered this dark and desperate world, died in our place, defeated death, in order to give humanity HOPE. Our Creator knows how desperately we need him to rescue us from our sin and our false hopes.

Before my eyes were opened to the true gospel, I thought his love was conditional upon my performance. My hope for acceptance and righteousness was in my own ability to earn salvation.

- *If* I'm a "good girl," then God will love me.
- *If* I "clean up my act," then maybe he will forgive me.
- *If* I "change my ways," then Jesus will accept me.

You don't have to be Einstein to figure out that I wasn't very good at being good. So I did the math and assumed God could/would never love a girl like me. The problem with my logic was twofold:

1. Incredibly bad theology.
2. A classic example of misplaced hope.

The Bible says Christ died because we are 100 percent hopeless without him. Each one of us is desperate for his grace—whether we see it or not. Eugene Peterson's paraphrase perfectly explains our situation.

> This is how much God loved the world: He gave his Son, his one and only Son. And this is why: so that no one need be destroyed; by believing in him (Jesus) anyone can have a whole and lasting life. God didn't go to all the trouble of sending his Son merely to point an accusing finger, telling the world how bad it was. He came to help, to put the world right again. Anyone who trusts in him is acquitted; anyone who refuses to trust him has long since been under the death sentence without knowing it. And why? Because of that person's failure to believe in the one-of-a-kind Son of God when introduced to him. (John 3:16–18 *The Message*)

Finally I "got it." The gospel message proved a beacon of light pointing me to solid ground. Like a sailor lost at sea, I welcomed this sight. Due to my track record of rebellion and sin, I now understood that I didn't have a shred of hope of pleasing a holy God on my own. My *only* hope for acceptance was the free gift of salvation offered through faith in his Son, Jesus Christ.

Placing my faith in Jesus, my life was transformed from instability to confidence because of my relationship with him. This gospel message proved so powerful that the entire foundation of my existence changed by believing it. One of my favorite hymns "The Solid Rock" says it best:

> My hope is built on nothing less
> Than Jesus' blood and righteousness. . . .
> On Christ the solid Rock I stand;
> All other ground is sinking sand.

At last . . . solid ground! Friends, this is where my journey of hoping in God began. I say journey, because that is what the Christian life really is—a walk of faith. I'd love to end this chapter here and tell you, "My life has been absolutely perfect. Bliss. I've never wavered in my faith and I've consistently hoped in Jesus for the rest of my days." Girls, that would be a bigger lie than cellulite cream. The honest truth is this: I have more in common with the Israelites than I ever imagined. Every *single* day (pun definitely intended) I'm learning what it means to hope in God.

Becoming a Woman Who Hopes in God!

Sure, I fell head over heels in love with Jesus. Not only was he my solid Rock but also my Redeemer, Savior, Healer, Comforter, and Friend. The more I followed him, the more I loved him. He proved his faithfulness in my life time and time again. This much is true, but the temptation to trust in false hopes is still a battle for those of us who believe in Jesus Christ.

Believing God is more than just a one-time decision to walk an aisle, pray a prayer, get sprinkled, confirmed, or baptized. Faith is a daily, moment-to-moment activity of hoping in God. It took me awhile to get this memo. When I would sing that old hymn, "My hope is built on nothing less than Jesus' blood and righteousness," I thought early on that this truth only applied to my eternal destination. You know . . . my hope for heaven. What I didn't realize is that God is our only hope for EVERYTHING in this life *and* in the next!

- The air we breathe.
- The food we eat.
- The health we enjoy.
- The healing we desire.
- The love we crave.
- The security we need.

Yet, it took a full-blown meltdown for me to realize that I, like Israel, was a redeemed girl clinging to a false hope. Sure, I loved Jesus and trusted him with my life, but there was still this one thing I was holding on to. So . . . what was this false hope? Drum roll please . . . *marriage.*

Gulp. Confession complete.

During a season in which all of my closest friends met their Someone, it seemed that God somehow forgot me. This was a painful (and expensive) season. I went into a bit of despair; I struggled trying to believe that my future was going to be good. I looked up, and my circle of friends had doubled . . . with the addition of husbands. The more the merrier did not apply here. Of course, my girlfriends included me, but an awkward distance crept in, when I began to feel like only half of a whole. Who was going to dinner? The Smiths, the Wallaces, the Joneses, oh, and Marian.

Their joy created a commonality that left me on the outside of their marriage vortex. Unintentional, though palpably real. (The awkward moment when the check comes, the endless chatter about house hunting, the beginning of discussions about babies . . . all of this made my search for a new apartment, a roommate, and fixing my own flat tire become an unbearable chasm between us.) I was alone. Completely, surprisingly, and unintentionally alone. This was so not my plan. Now, my life felt hopeless. Because the one, THE ONE, had not come. Can we just say, "BIG LETDOWN!"

I was undone, falling apart. Serious crazy place. During a time of prayer (translation: snotty sob fest with Bible close by and Jesus is the recipient of my pathetic pleas), the Lord led me to Psalm 33. Here, he showed me the root of my despair—my misplaced hope.

This was so not my plan.

I was still just a girl looking for my Prince Charming to come along and "rescue" me. In that season, I shifted my hope from the person of Jesus to the person who would propose marriage . . . trading the One and Only for "the One."

Here's the thing, Jesus loves you and me too much to just sit back and let us hope in something that won't deliver. Any married girl out there can tell you, husbands don't provide happiness. This may come as a shock, but marriage isn't the solution to all of life's woes for a single girl. Hear me out, I'm not saying marriage isn't a wonderful blessing—it is. I'm just confessing that my problem was that I was placing my *expectation* for my future in someone other than Jesus, and as a result the massive boulders of despair and disappointment rolled in, crushing me under their weight.

Therefore, at the top of God's List is his desire that we become women who believe and hope *in him*, now. In doing so, we become a beacon of light to others who are desperate without him.

When God showed me the truth in Psalm 33, not only did I recognize my false hope, but I also discovered the profile of a woman who hopes in God. "The *eyes of the LORD* are on those who fear him, on those whose *hope is in his unfailing love, to deliver them* from death and keep them alive in famine" (vv. 18–19 NIV, emphasis mine). There are three aspects of this verse that describe a woman who hopes in God. First, she believes "the eyes of the Lord" are upon her. Second, she "hopes in his unfailing love." Finally, she knows "he will deliver."

The Eyes of the Lord

One of the tricky things about teaching God's word is the fact that I'm always tested on the subject before I can teach it to others. Today is a test of hope. Every time I turn on the news or see a headline, I hear the same thing—economy crashing, gas prices soaring, swine-flu spreading, food shortage—and on and on ring the alarms of pending doom. It is quite easy to lose hope in a world where terrorism reigns, morals decline, and humanity suffers.

I am the first to admit that we, as Americans, live incredibly comfortable lives compared to the rest of the world. Tune into the news, and you are immersed in stories of widespread hunger, poverty related diseases, and senseless deaths. In my sterilized niche of the world, I've never had to think about where my next meal will come from—nor does the idea seem appealing. I know we are materially blessed, and I know we are not entitled to these blessings. I am acutely aware that at any time these warnings could become a reality.

Each time I hear these reports I'm faced with a decision. Freak out or believe God. Seriously, fear is the air we breathe these days. As a single girl, with a single income, the temptation to fear the future is always present. The questions roll in:

- What will happen when the economy does take a nosedive?
- What will happen if there is a food famine in our country?
- How will I survive if people are more concerned with buying bread than buying books?
- What will I do if I never marry and it's just me . . . and the cat I don't even own yet?

The questions are real. The questions cause me to pause. The questions cause me to ask myself a serious question: *Do I really believe "the eyes of the Lord" are on me?* Do I really believe he is faithfully watching over me to provide, to protect, and to preserve? Do I really believe he is all-knowing and perceives my needs from afar? Do I really believe in the God David described in Psalm 23?

The LORD is *my* shepherd;
>   there is nothing I lack.
He lets me lie down in green pastures;
>   He leads me beside quiet waters.
He renews my life;
>   He leads me along the right paths
>   for His name's sake.
Even when I go
>   through the darkest valley,
>   I fear no danger,
>   for You are with me;
>   Your rod and Your staff—
>   they comfort me.
You prepare a table before me
>   in the presence of my enemies;
>   You anoint my head with oil;
>   my cup overflows.
>   Only goodness and faithful love
>   will pursue me
>   all the days of my life,
>   and I will dwell in the house of the LORD
>   as long as I live.

Unlike King David, who wrote of the Lord lovingly leading his own, many people perceive God as distant, cold, removed. Not involved in the day-to-day affairs of this world. No wonder they feel hopeless when tragedy strikes or when life doesn't make sense—their God is absent. Not my God. Not the God of the Bible.

He is the with-us, never-leave-or-forsake-us, move-the-mountains, loving-Shepherd-who-watches-over-his-flock kind of God.

Today, by God's grace, I can face those scary questions with confidence. I've experienced his provision, his power, and his protection. I have peace and joy because my expectation for the future is in the Lord, for I know his eye is on me.

Hope in His Unfailing Love

Unbelief is one of the hardest obstacles to overcome in a woman's heart. Doubts and fears lead some women to control and others to despair but both types of women are plagued by unbelief. So many women who are redeemed by the grace of Jesus Christ struggle with fear because they don't truly believe God loves them. At the core of their being, they doubt God's goodness—and wonder if his intentions for them are good.

I so understand! At one point in my Christian walk, I, too, struggled with the same doubts. Though I experienced salvation and knew my sins were forgiven—still, I wrestled with believing that God loved *me*. Not global God love, but that he loved me—*just me*. So, this kind of doubt made it difficult to hope in God, because frankly, I didn't trust that God really gave a flip about me. Our Enemy loves to play this card; he absolutely hates it when a child of God is confident in his love for her.

Picture a three-year-old little girl standing at the edge of a swimming pool. Her favorite floaties tossed aside. It's just her, the big pool, and Daddy in the water standing a frightening two feet away. Her fear is great . . . especially without the security of her floaties. She stands at the edge, eyeing the water just inches below, when her daddy says, "Come on, sweetheart. Jump to me. I'll catch you." She hesitates. And then, with all the might her little body can muster, she propels herself into her father's arms—her feet skimming the water along the way.

Do you know what happened in that split second she hesitated? She asked herself these questions: *Does my daddy love me? Will my daddy catch me? Can I trust him?* Her answer wasn't said in words, but in a leap—the leap from the safety of the ledge to the security of her daddy's arms. She hoped he would catch her because she believed he loved her. As one of my favorite Scriptures says, "There is no fear in love; instead, perfect love drives out fear" (1 John 4:18). When we understand how perfect God's love for us is, then our fears and our doubts are banished in light of the truth.

Girls, the miracle of our hope in Jesus is that we become children of God. Now, we are not the recipients of only his grace but also his fatherly love, care, and provision. Check out these amazing truths and ask God to help you believe these promises—not just with your head but with your heart.

I AM A CHILD OF GOD!

Yet to all who received him [Jesus], to those who believed in his name, he gave the right to become children of God—children born not of natural descent, nor of human decision or a husband's will, but born of God. (John 1:12–13 NIV)

MY HEAVENLY FATHER LOVES ME!

How great is the love the Father has lavished on us, that we should be called children of God! And that is what we are! The reason the world does not know us is that it did not know him. (1 John 3:1 NIV)

I AM BLESSED AND FAVORED IN CHRIST!

Blessed be the God and Father of our Lord Jesus Christ, who has blessed us with every spiritual blessing in the heavens, in Christ; for He chose us in Him, before the foundation of the world, to be holy and blameless in His sight. In love He predestined us to be adopted through Jesus Christ for Himself, according to His favor and will, to the praise of His glorious grace that He favored us with in the Beloved. (Eph. 1:3–6)

I HAVE A GLORIOUS INHERITANCE IN CHRIST!

I pray that the eyes of your heart may be enlightened so you may know what is the hope of His calling, what are the glorious riches of His inheritance among the saints. (Eph. 1:18)

GOD'S POWER WORKS FOR ME, HIS CHILD!

I pray also that the eyes of your heart may be enlightened in order that you may know . . . his incomparably great power for us who believe. That power is like the working of his mighty strength, which he exerted in Christ when he raised him from the dead and seated him at his right hand in the heavenly realms. (Eph. 1:18–20 NIV)

NOTHING CAN SEPARATE ME FROM GOD'S LOVE!

For I am persuaded that neither death nor life, nor angels nor rulers, nor things present, nor things to come, nor powers, nor height, nor depth, nor any other created thing will have the power to separate us from the love of God that is in Christ Jesus our Lord! (Rom. 8:38–39)

The woman who hopes in God believes her identity as a child of God: loved, chosen, called, empowered, equipped, protected, sealed, shielded, and blessed. The Father's love for you is unfailing. Don't allow unbelief to keep you from the confident assurance that is yours as a daughter of the King!

To Deliver

I just finished lunch with one of my favorite college coeds. Her testimony is very similar to my own. She had a wild past, but God has redeemed and restored her life. Over our carb-packed lunch of pizza and french fries, we discussed the all-important topics of boys and dating.

My friend has a new crush . . . a Big Crush! She is smitten, if you know what I mean. So, we are chatting along and she's detailing to me their "friendship" and how she hopes to see this young man again soon (he lives three states away) . . . and really hopes that "he's the one."

So, as I'm apt to do in a moment like this, I ask what is to me, the most important question: Tell me about his relationship with Jesus.

Pause.

Awkward silence.

Muttering and mumbling.

Cough.

"I'm sorry," I ask, now a little confused, "what was that you just said? He's a 'really good guy but not necessarily a follower of Jesus'?"

> **She grew tired of waiting on the Lord to provide Mr. Right and decided to take matters into her own hands and date Mr. Right now.**

As she looks up sheepishly from her pizza, the full story unfolds.

My friend looked around her university and didn't see any godly men pursuing Jesus who were also pursuing her. So, she grew tired of waiting on the Lord to provide Mr. Right and decided to take matters into her own hands and date Mr. Right *now*. She convinced herself that it was just a temporary fling—a summer crush.

The problem with this rationalization is that our hearts don't always get the "don't fall for this guy memo." When we spend time with someone, it is very easy to fall for him. And now, my sweet friend, who loves Jesus, has fallen for a guy who doesn't share her values *or* her God.

How did this happen? She explained that she began doubting whether or not God *really* cared about the desires of her heart. She reasoned she might as well date this guy, who was clearly interested in her, because "God may not deliver."

Most women reading this understand her struggle. You long for something, and the waiting becomes oh-so-difficult. To hope in God is choosing to believe he will deliver. A woman who hopes in God trusts him to provide for her needs. She commits the desires of her heart to him, confident that his plan and his timing are best.

What are you waiting on God to deliver? Are you setting your hope on Jesus or trusting in something or someone else to meet your needs? Or perhaps, like my friend, you've decided to take matters into your own hands. Friends, hope in God. There are amazing blessings in store for those of us who do. He desires good for you. Don't settle. Hear the Lord speak this promise to you.

> Why do you say . . .
> "My way is hidden from the LORD;
> my cause is disregarded by my God"?
> Do you not know?
> Have you not heard?

The LORD is the everlasting God,
the Creator of the ends of the earth.
He will not grow tired or weary,
and his understanding no one can fathom.
He gives strength to the weary
and increases the power of the weak.
Even youths grow tired and weary,
and young men stumble and fall;
but those who hope in the LORD
will renew their strength.
They will soar on wings like eagles;
they will run and not grow weary,
they will walk and not be faint.
(Isa. 40:27–31 NIV)

Trust me when I tell you that I KNOW how tempting it is to take matters in your own hands when waiting on a desire of your heart to be fulfilled. Friend, if there is one thing I know for sure from my season of singleness it's this: God knows our hearts' desires far better than we do. The last thing we want is to settle for anything that is not his best for us. When we choose to hope in God, we trust that he will deliver the very best . . . in his way and in his timing. I could fill this book with testimony after testimony of women who waited and trusted in God. He proved his faithfulness in their lives. Never settle!

I See a Generation

Recently, I spoke these truths to a group of college and young single women—girls who daily face the temptation to hope in a guy, in their grades, or in getting the perfect job for their future security. These girls are smack-dab in the middle of the season of life that defines for most women where their hope will be placed. I've heard it said many times that between ages eighteen and twenty-eight the most important decisions in life are made. The audience seated before me was in the midst of that pivotal season—a time when each will decide whether or not she will hope in God.

After explaining the truth about false hopes and presenting Jesus as the only one worthy of our hope, I found myself choked up with tears. I'm not much of a crier—so this emotion was genuine. Welling up inside of me was an overwhelming thankfulness for the past and a longing for the future.

> **As a single girl, I've watched the Lord provide, protect, lead, direct, defend, and strengthen me in ways I never would have known had I been married.**

Thankfulness . . . I'm infinitely grateful that the Lord delivered me from my false hopes—the self-made, material longings and plans that I had trusted in and that could never provide fulfillment. I wept before these women because I was overwhelmed by God's goodness. My words fail to explain to you how incredibly grateful I am that God did not give me my plan. While I still have desires, I now see my season of singleness as an amazing blessing. As a single girl, I've watched the Lord provide, protect, lead, direct, defend, and strengthen me in ways I never would have known had I been married.

I know his eye is on me.

I know his love is unfailing.

I know he delivers.

Longing . . . for a generation of women who love and profess faith in Jesus, to actually *hope* in Jesus. As I looked out over the hundreds of young women seated before me, I felt the urgency of the hour. Will we become women who hope in the Lord? Or will we continue to follow the path of the world, trusting our lives to empty and disappointing false hopes?

God is calling us out. God is seeking a generation of women who hope in him. God is raising up his daughters to stand as lights in this dark world—women who tell the hopeless where real hope is found. Are you that woman? Psalm 33 concludes with the anthem of a woman who chooses to hope in God. Friends, I challenge you to say these words aloud with me. Make this your anthem and confession as you choose during your single season to become a woman who hopes in God.

> *We wait in hope for the LORD; he is our help and our shield. In him our hearts rejoice, for we trust in his holy name. May your unfailing love rest upon us, O LORD, even as we put our hope in you.*
>
> Psalm 33:20–22 NIV

— NUMBER 3 —

Pursue Beauty

To make your season
beautiful,
become a girl who reflects
the Beautiful One!

For attractive lips, speak words of kindness.
For lovely eyes, seek out good in people.
For a slim figure, share your food with the hungry.
For poise, walk with the knowledge you'll never walk alone.
—AUDREY HEPBURN

The Wall

Image after image of toned bodies, perfect hair, flawless complexions, and expertly applied makeup lined my bathroom wall in high school. Magazine cutouts, one after another, forming a giant collage of beauty—a virtual wallpaper of airbrushed models, posing in the latest trends and designer garb, stared back at me as I meticulously applied the prescribed amounts of mascara, blush, and lip gloss.

> My List *demanded* beauty. How else would I find acceptance? How else would I meet Mr. Right? How else would I earn popularity? How else would I feel happy?

This wall, carefully constructed from various fashion magazines through my teen years, embodied the look of a "beautiful" woman. (Or rather the fashion industry's current measure of beauty.) Her eyes, her lips, her smile, her hair . . . these cover girls were *the standard, the definer, the measuring stick* for the woman I wanted to become. The woman I *must* become. After all, friends, my List *demanded* beauty. How else would I find acceptance? How else would I meet Mr. Right? How else would I earn popularity? How else would I feel happy?

Every day, as I dressed for school, the wall spoke to me . . . it guided me: Buy this, wear this, eat this, apply this, beauty is this. I listened. I watched. I learned. For, you see, I longed for beauty. Fortunately, my wall of glossy magazine images told me "how to become beautiful."

- Quick steps to "kissable lips"
- The best hairstyle for your face shape
- Workouts that work
- Bikini body in thirty days
- Sexiest hair ever
- Lose weight fast
- Five-minute abs

Ironically, as I passionately pursued external beauty, I was missing the key ingredient—a beautiful heart. Looking back on those years, I know one thing for sure: I was *not* a beautiful girl. No, I'm not feeling insecure and bashing how God created me. I'm just being honest about the nature

> As I passionately pursued external beauty, I was missing the key ingredient—a beautiful heart.

of the girl I used to be: angry, bitter, selfish, insecure, jealous, catty, argumentative, cold, hard, spoiled, complaining, prideful, defensive, and a teensy bit controlling.

Whew, I'm out of breath, but the list could be longer. Seriously, it really didn't matter what I did to transform the outside because on the inside, I was not so pretty. In fact, I was downright ugly. The hardness of my heart was barely containable. I may have been considered pretty until I opened my mouth, but once I opened my mouth, the hours of primping, grooming, curling, painting, plucking, and brushing disappeared. I, like the images I longed to reflect, was nothing but a "plastic."

Beauty is wrapped up in the condition of the heart. Inner beauty creates outer beauty. Or, maybe more simply put, a woman is even more attractive or beautiful if, first, her heart is "beautiful."
—Jeff, age 28

A Parade of Plastic

The term "the Plastics" was first introduced to American pop culture with the hit movie *Mean Girls*.[1] In this film, Lindsay Lohan stars as Cady (pronounced Katie), who is a sweet, sheltered, formerly homeschooled teenager, who spent most of her childhood in Africa with her parents. When her parents move back to America her junior year of high school, Cady is plunged into the world of catty and competitive high school social battles, which she often parallels to animal behavior in the African wild.

The first friends she makes, Janis and Damian, are hardly part of the in crowd, but they accept her and have an easy friendship. When the reigning queens of the popular kids, the Plastics, show interest in Cady, Janis comes up with a plan to take revenge against the girls who "ruined her life," using Cady as an inside agent.

The word *plastic* is used metaphorically to describe these girls because their beauty is only external and artificial. In the film, the three most popular girls in school seem perfect on the outside but are fake on the inside. Sure, the Plastics are pretty by all accounts. Their immaculate outfits (that nobody else has, of course) are draped flawlessly over their perfect figures, topped with perfect hair and pageant smiles. They walk through school, arms linked together, in synchronized steps, ready to be admired, loved, and of course, envied.

The Plastics often say one thing to someone's face but then talk about that person ruthlessly behind her back, saying nasty and *mean* things. Hence, the title *Mean Girls*. They gossip, fight, argue, manipulate, scheme, lie, and put down one another in their effort to be the queen bees or most popular girls in school. The result is not so pretty.

> The term *plastic* has become synonymous with a girl who's extremely attractive on the outside, yet empty and shallow on the inside—a type of beauty that's literally only skin deep.

Cady is all for the plan to take down the queen bee of the Plastics, Regina George. The plan contains several points of attack, including ruining Regina's perfect body and helping end the relationship with her "hottie" boyfriend (the one she's already cheating on). Ironically, the more Cady gets involved with the Plastics (even as a secret reputation assassin), the more she becomes like them. She transforms from kind to catty in weeks. By adopting their style, she inherits their substance. She moves from being the innocent, smart, and genuine girl to someone who rivals Regina in manipulation and shallowness.

Today, the term *plastic* has become synonymous with a girl who's extremely attractive on the outside, yet empty and shallow on the inside—a type of beauty that's literally only skin deep. It seems that as more focus is placed on external beauty, the uglier the heart can become. Please hear me when I say that there are plenty of externally beautiful women who are just as beautiful on the inside. I know plenty of women with head-turning looks and beautiful hearts. My point is that when we are tempted to fixate on our outer beauty only (skin, hair, makeup, outfit, size), the result is that we are focusing exclusively on ourselves. This fight for the perfect look is a losing battle with casualties named kindness, goodness, gentleness, and selflessness.

Sadly, women in our culture are flat out pursuing external beauty at record speeds. Check out the numbers for the United States in just 2007:

- Nearly 3 million Botox injections were distributed.
- The average American woman spent between $12,000 and $15,000 on beauty-related purchases. (Yes, I said $15,000—that is a car, ladies.)
- More than 11 million cosmetic surgical and nonsurgical procedures were performed.
- A half million women in the United States underwent liposuction.
- Since 1997 (over the previous ten years), surgical procedures increased 142 percent, while nonsurgical procedures (botox, injections, laser treatments) increased 743 percent.[2]

But, after all the nips and tucks, are we really more beautiful than before? Sure, we might turn a few more heads, but does this type of beauty capture a heart? If you're a single girl like me, you know how hard it is not to get caught up in all the craziness . . . the bombardment of messages telling us how to become sexy, hot, and wanted. But just look around; are women today *really* more beautiful?

Real Beauty

In contrast to the plastic culture that results from our tireless pursuit of external beauty stands the classic *Jane Eyre*. I recently became somewhat obsessed with this Charlotte Brontë novel. My mild obsession began after reading it again this past winter (it had been a very long time since my high school British lit class). And, as you know, I am a huge Jane Austen fan, so on a recent trip to Blockbuster, I happened upon the BBC version of *Jane Eyre*, and all I can say is, un-be-liev-able. So very, very good. I digress. (But seriously, you should rent it soon.)

Watching *Jane Eyre*, I realized that women today can learn a great deal about real beauty from her character—*character* being the key word here.

Jane is an orphaned girl in England in the mid-1800s. Completely alone and without inheritance or social stature, Jane is adopted by her aunt and uncle after her parents' deaths. Her aunt breaks the promise to her dying husband to care and provide for Jane, only to neglect, berate, belittle, and banish the young girl. Rejected and reviled, Jane Eyre is sent away to a school for girls where she excels in academics and becomes an accomplished artist and musician. These skills prepare her to become a teacher or, in her case, a governess for wealthy children who are schooled on their families' estates.

Jane is hired by the Rochester family and taken to Thornfield Hall, a brooding castle above the English highlands. Within this estate are servants, the lord and master of the manor, Mr. Rochester, and his ward, Adele—a little French girl whom Jane Eyre is to educate. There is very little emotion or love within the walls of the castle.

Jane is plain. Her appearance is described as "unremarkable." By the standards of the day, she has no "specialty." Her hair is dark, she is not tall, she is thin, she is pale. She wears dark, modest dresses and shows only a bit of a fashion flare when she ties a red scarf around the neckline of her gray wool dress for special occasions. But Jane has something extraordinary—a magical quality that's hard to define. She is smart, kind, nurturing, loyal, and strong. Gifted at languages, science, and music, she has the ability to communicate with all walks of life—nobility, servants, children, adults, missionaries, and mediums. She speaks plainly and from the heart. As she often states, "I know who I am." And the lord of the manor (the Prince Charming of this tale) is riveted.

Why? Could it be that she's beautiful to him? Are her charms and her features transcendent of fashion and face? I submit to you this theory: Jane reflects the fruits of the spirit—gentleness, kindness, self-control, etc., and Prince Charming is enthralled on a completely different level.

As the story unfolds, we are introduced to the beautiful Blanche, who by all popular accounts is the belle of the county. She is tall and blonde, wears oodles of chiffon and lace, and has boingy curls and a noble family. She is flirtatious and sly, bold, and beautiful. She is catty and controlling and bores quickly if all attention is not focused on her. She rides horseback like the wind with her dresses of gorgeous taffeta billowing behind her, etching a band of beauty across the English countryside. From afar, she is magnificent. We meet her because Lord Rochester is in pursuit of a wife, and everyone assumes Blanche will be his choice.

Yet, scene after scene reveals his growing boredom and distaste with the vapid conversations of the noble and the heartless pursuits of the well-bred, their trivial games played in the parlor. Blanche is exposed as vain, empty, and shallow. Instead of falling for her charms, Mr. Rochester seeks out the company of Jane. He delights in her humor, honesty, forthright approach to all things trivial and important. She loves and nurtures Adele. She encourages her and is kind and respectful to those in society who outwardly scorn her. All of this to say . . . he falls in love with her, and she with him.

As the story ends, and I am so sorry to spoil it if you haven't read/seen it yet, but I must make this point: Prince Charming loses his sight. He is blind. And he and Jane are reunited after a season of separation. In his darkened world, she radiates true beauty revealing high-quality character that cannot be seen with eyes but rather is observed within the soul and felt within the heart. I am reminded of the description of love in 1 Corinthians 13: Jane is patient and kind. Not jealous or conceited or proud. Jane doesn't keep a record of wrongdoings. And so they live, happily ever after, blinded to fad, fame, and fortune, attracted to the beauty that only Christ within can radiate, connected by a loveliness that does not fade with time.

Reflecting the Beautiful One

How does a woman become beautiful? Simple. She reflects the beautiful One. Who is the beautiful One? His name is Jesus—the One whose beauty has captivated sinners and drawn billions from death to life. In my pursuit of beauty, the Lord has taught me three words—a simple three-step process for becoming a beautiful girl. I'm the first to admit that I'm still very much in process, but I'm happy to say I do know the secret.

Abide . . . Behold . . . Become . . .

The first word is *abide*. Abiding in Jesus is the first step to real beauty—the kind of beauty that really matters. To abide means to remain connected to him. We see this word in the vine and branch illustration Jesus gave his disciples the night before his crucifixion. He said, "Abide in Me, and I in you. As the branch cannot bear fruit of itself unless it abides in the vine, so neither can you unless you abide in Me. I am the vine, you are the branches; he who abides in Me and I in him, he bears much fruit, for apart from Me you can do nothing" (John 15:4–5 NASB). Just as the branch must stay connected to the vine for life and to produce fruit, so we

78

must stay connected to Jesus if our lives will produce the beautiful fruit of his Spirit.

How do we stay connected? First of all, we must spend time *daily* in his Word, the Bible. Jesus said, "If you abide in Me, and My words abide in you, ask whatever you wish, and it will be done for you. My Father is glorified by this, that you bear much fruit, and so prove to be My disciples" (John 15:7–8 NASB). When a woman spends consistent time in the Word of God, she is connected to Christ. His words fill her. His words guide her. His words shape her. As a result, his fruit is seen in her.

What is this fruit Jesus is referring to? It is the fruit of the Spirit, or rather, the character qualities of a beautiful woman. When we remain connected to Jesus, he produces his life in and through us—the overflow of his Spirit. In Galatians 5:22–23, the fruit is described as "love, joy, peace, patience, kindness, goodness, faithfulness, gentleness, and self-control" (NIV).

So, how does *abiding* produce such beautiful bounty? I'm so glad you asked. That takes us to our second word—*behold*. Girls, when we abide in Jesus, we *behold* his beautiful character. We see how Christ responds to the ugliness of this world, and his glorious nature shines through us. In the Psalms, King David described this type of abiding relationship: "One thing I have asked from the LORD, that I shall seek: that I may dwell in the house of the LORD all the days of my life, to behold the beauty of the LORD and to meditate in His temple" (Ps. 27:4 NASB, emphasis mine). In the Bible's original language, Hebrew, the same word David uses here for "dwell" is translated in the New Testament by John as "abide." Both passages teach us the same principle.

When we abide, remain, or dwell in God's presence, we behold his beauty and by beholding we *become* more beautiful. We are women transformed in his presence. Second Corinthians 3:18 explains this process of abiding, beholding, and becoming: "We all, with unveiled face, beholding as in a mirror the glory of the Lord, are being transformed into the same image from glory to glory, just as from the Lord, the Spirit" (NASB, emphasis mine). As we behold the Beautiful One, we in turn become beautiful. His Spirit fills us. His life empowers us. His Word transforms us. His character conforms us to his image.

> When we abide, remain, or dwell in God's presence, we behold his beauty and by beholding we become more beautiful. We are women transformed in his presence.

The most beautiful women I know are ones who know this secret. They aren't striving to perfect some external beauty, but, instead, are women who choose to abide in Jesus and reflect to the world *his* beautiful character.

Over the years I've learned a great beauty secret. No, it is not the latest and greatest body cleanse or turn-back-the-clock facial. I've discovered that if I want to be a woman who reflects the Beautiful One, I absolutely must devote the first portion of my day to beholding him. As I survey my friends and encounter breath-taking women around the world, I've learned that women who have the beautiful Christlike character I desire are women who devote the first of their day to beholding Jesus. I suppose these are my new role models. Gone are the plastic images from my high school days; now I admire women whose lives are filled with grace, kindness, gentleness, love, and truth. Their beauty secret is time with Jesus, and I've learned from watching their lives how transformational this time really is.

I now consider this portion of my day just as essential as brushing my teeth or applying the can't-leave-home-without-it mascara. My quiet time (praying and reading God's Word) is far more beneficial than any time spent primping, plucking, brushing, grooming, or painting in transforming me into the woman God considers beautiful.[3] Trust me, I'm seriously ugly left to my natural state—I'm not a "roll-out-of-bed-beautiful" kind of girl. I must abide. I must behold. I must become more like Jesus and less like Marian every single day.

Turn Your Eyes upon Jesus

When I think of the process of **abiding, beholding, and becoming,** my mind wanders to the old hymn, "Turn Your Eyes upon Jesus." The lyrics perfectly describe the activity of beholding the Beautiful One:

> Turn your eyes upon Jesus,
> Look full in His wonderful face;
> And the things of earth will grow strangely dim
> In the light of His glory and grace.[4]

Looking fully into the face of Jesus, a woman's countenance is transformed. For she is looking directly into the eyes of unconditional love. She knows she is accepted . . . therefore she is freed from the need to compete and strive in hopes of finding acceptance. She knows

> **Looking fully into the face of Jesus, a woman's countenance is transformed. For she is looking directly into the eyes of unconditional love.**

she is adored . . . therefore she is freed from the need to conform to worldly standards of beauty because she is confident in whom God created her to be. She knows she is secure . . . therefore she is freed from the worries and fears that plague those who don't rest in his loving care. Yes, when a woman turns her eyes on Jesus, the things of this world do grow strangely dim—the very things that end up causing our wrinkles, driving us to overeat, stressing our bodies, and depleting the natural beauty God has given us.

Let me just say for the record, I'm not immune to the maddening messages women face every single day. Just this week I contemplated the benefits of Botox, the pros and cons of liposuction, the downside of gravity (pun intended), and the emergence of something called a "muffin top."

Tammy Wynette said it best, "Sometimes it's hard to be a woman!"

As I walk through the supermarket, I see the magazine covers; as I ride in a taxi, I hear radio hosts ragging on celebs looking "over-the-hill"; and as I get dressed some mornings, I look in the mirror and hear that old voice whisper back at me, "You are not good enough."

There is definitely still a girl inside of me who would love to perfect all her flaws and prevent her inevitable sagging future. I, too, live in this world where thirty is old and old is ugly. But you know what, a different voice speaks to me now, and that is the voice of the Beautiful One. Every morning Jesus tells me who I am. He tells me that "charm is deceptive and beauty is fleeting, but a woman who fears the Lord shall be praised" (Prov. 31:30). He tells me to seek his face. He reminds me of what really matters. He reminds me that a beautiful heart is far more pleasing to him than an airbrushed face.

Everyday I'm choosing to listen to the voice of Jesus because I want to live for his glory. Sure, I still put on my favorite mascara and I still fight the frizz, but I don't live any longer for a wall of plastic images. I'm free . . . free to be who God created *me* to be.

A Guy's Perspective

Girls, I may be a blonde, but I'm no fool. I realize that when attempting to persuade a bunch of single women to pursue internal beauty instead of external beauty, it's going to take more than a little persuading. So, I thought to myself, "Marian, you're a single girl. What would it take to persuade *you* to pursue real beauty?" I pondered my question oh-so-briefly before snapping my fingers and saying, "Aha! They'll need a guy's perspective!"

So, ladies, without further ado, I present to you a guy's perspective. Not only is the following advice from a man, but this (single) guy also happens to be a male model. (Yes, as in chiseled, tan, gorgeous, and godly.) So don't you dare take my word for it on the subject of beauty; I offer you the words of my friend (yes, I promise we're 100 percent just friends) Bryan Mitchell.

Dear Women Everywhere:

I am a male model. I've worked as a model in the fashion industry for over fourteen years. One question I am frequently asked is, "Do you work with a lot of beautiful women?" Sometimes, if I don't feel like talking, and knowing that they're really just talking about physical appearance, I acknowledge and say yes. Other times, when I sense it may be helpful, I express what I always think and feel when people ask that question, and my response is, "Sadly, not so much."

When guys ask the question they tend to use the word "hot," and it's obvious what they are asking. But women tend to use the word "beautiful," and I think this reveals a common misconception—the confusion in our culture about what makes a woman beautiful. Sure, in my business, there are plenty of physically attractive women. They are often told how good-looking they are, and experience certain perks as they are pursued by men and afforded opportunities and privileges that others might not be. So if you follow the common cultural mind-set, you might expect everything for them to be great. Instead, you find in these women a lot of insecurity, jealousy, and striving. Their character and countenance proves anything but attractive.

Do you realize that 100 percent of the women you see on the covers of magazines are photo-shopped? Do you know what that is? It is a computer graphics program that provides instant plastic surgery. Even better, it also provides perfect lighting, enhanced colors, and feathering around any skin imperfections. It is the advertising industry's magic wand.

And so in my industry, it's painfully obvious to all of the men that the cover look is not something attainable. We know that the women don't really look like that, and being objects of photoshopping ourselves, we know it's an impossibility to attain.

Don't get me wrong. These women are great-looking, or at least possess a certain something that the advertiser is looking for, but they ARE NOT PERFECT. They are a compilation of the image that the advertiser wants to convey. And what most men and I are looking for is someone real. Real people have real skin, real noses, real eyelashes, real hair . . . and, yes, perhaps a bit of body fat. Ironically, as a single man, I always hear women say that they want a guy who loves them for "who they are." Yet, I see these same women striving and conforming to the latest trends.

> When a woman is walking with Jesus, she can't help but reflect HIS glory.

Real beauty, in my opinion, is a condition of the heart, not the face. Eyes that are bright, a smile that is genuine, joy that produces a glow. I am not above turning my head in the direction of a stunning woman, but what keeps my focus is how she carries herself. Is she kind? Is she confident? Is she gentle? Is she joyful? Does she have integrity? If so, she is exemplifying fruits of the Spirit. You can spot these girls, you know. The ones who have gazed upon true Beauty, in the form of Jesus Christ. And they are radiant from their encounter. When a woman is walking with Jesus, she can't help but reflect HIS glory. She is a joy to be around, she is a safe place to entrust your confidences, and she is a mighty warrior in times of trouble. If we define beauty only in terms of external appearance, then beautiful women in our culture are easily replaceable and have a very limited shelf life. On the other hand, if we understand beauty in a much deeper more meaningful sense, then a woman who is beautiful is one a man might seek after with all his heart, and when he finds her he sees her as completely irreplaceable.

In my business, fads and trends are what make the industry go 'round and 'round. The fashion industry, beauty magazines, product commercials, and trendsetters exist to define beauty and manipulate insecurities. If what is cool today is still cool two years from now, then people won't buy as much stuff. So people are continually led to believe that they need the newest, hottest in thing. This creates an unending and exhausting hamster wheel.

Many of you have been on this wheel for a long time and experiencing the futility of it. My hope for you is that you might pursue the Beautiful One, Jesus, because he is worth pursuing. When you do, you will experience the transforming power of his grace in your life, and it will manifest itself through you in a way that could only be described as beautiful.

> *"Charm is deceptive and beauty is fleeting, but a woman who fears the Lord will be praised."*
> —Proverbs 31:30

Seek First

To make your season
beautiful, become a girl
who passionately pursues
the kingdom of God.

Seek first the kingdom of God . . .
and all these things will be provided for you.
—JESUS (MATT. 6:33)

Struggling

She's twenty-seven . . . ish. All of her friends think she's a catch. She is smart, fun, and loves God. Like many of you reading this book, she hears the same thing all the time, "I can't believe you are still single!" This is a girl who lives out her faith, but if you were to ask her today, she'd tell you she is seriously struggling. Struggling with what she's supposed to do in this surprising season called singleness.

She's read all the books. You know, the plethora of guides for us single girls, instructing us on how to:

- Find *the one.*
- Become *the one.*
- And keep *the one.*

Frankly, she's frustrated because she's still "just one." It seems none of these so-called guides have changed her status.

Her most recent boyfriend ended their relationship with the crushing words, "I'd rather just be friends." Ouch! Of course, this was *not* her plan. To her dismay, she now faces another wedding season without even a prospect of a date. I can feel her pain and the sheer revulsion I have for the bouquet toss and the awkward "singles" table just thinking about it.

Oh, the horror!

The Question

I encountered this girl a few weeks after her breakup and just days into her own full-blown meltdown. (P.S. Here's a little FYI about yours truly—I am known around my city as a bit of an expert on handling women in meltdown mode. Like the National Guard during a hurricane, I'm called in for broken engagements, ex-boyfriends' weddings, turning-thirty freak-outs, and your run-of-the-mill "he-broke-my-heart-and-now-I'm-going-to-be-single-until-rapture" moments. It's a gift . . . what can I say?)

Where was I? Oh, yes . . . triage.

Post-breakup triage is how I acquired my most recent case. She and I meet to talk, and due to the fact that I have experience in prolonged singleness and the how-to-put-your-life-back-together-again-after-crushing-breakup department, she looks up at me through tears and asks me an extremely crucial question: "What am I supposed to do with my life . . . *now?*"

Allow me to translate what this question *really* means. My friend wants to know:

- What am I supposed to do *now* that I'm single?
- What do I live for *now* that I don't have a man in my life, much less the prospect of one?
- What do I do with myself *now* that I don't have my List?

Friends, it's living in "now" that can be difficult for us, isn't it?

Over the last few years I've encountered hundreds of young women who fit my friend's description. They are twenty-ish, thirty-ish, and dare I say it . . . forty-ish, and still single (or single again), and many are asking the "now" question. They do love Jesus, but *their List* is nowhere to be found; therefore, they are confused, disillusioned, and frankly, feeling a little bit lost. Aside from the loneliness and disappointment, most of them just want to know what they are supposed to do . . . in the meantime. You know, that span of time between graduation and getting hitched.

One thing God wired into us girls is the ability to plan. Face it, we can set an agenda. Most of us have decided what we will do, where we will go, and what shoes we will wear with what outfit for the next year. Women adore a schedule, a plan, or a program. This ability comes in super handy for the multitasking gender. Yet, the problem arises when our plans don't pan out. That is precisely the moment when most of us begin to *totally* freak out.

> **Women adore a schedule, a plan, or a program. . . . The problem arises when our plans don't pan out.**

I'm sure many of you reading this feel like I did a few years ago. It seemed like most of my friends had gotten their ticket to Marriedville, but I had somehow missed the train and was now stuck in Singlecity. Obviously, the teenager who penned the List did not have the foresight to include a clause that read "prolonged season of singleness"; therefore, I was off track, wingin' it without a plan. (Cue: Freak out.) Thankfully, God showed me the next item on his List, which just happens to be the answer to the "now" question.

Seek First

"Seek first the kingdom of God and His righteousness, and all these things will be provided for you" (Matt. 6:33). Although this verse is one of the most often quoted, printed, and memorized Scriptures, I daresay that actually putting this one into practice is quite different from merely memorizing the words. Let's break this one down a bit, shall we?

Seek ...
strive, pursue, or chase after with intensity

First ...
your chief and primary objective

The kingdom ...
the realm of rule and authority

of God ...
where God, our Creator and Savior reigns!

God revealed to me that by seeking *first* his kingdom agenda, then all things I longed for and desired would ultimately be added to my life. The trick is to get the order right. Most of us have the order reversed. The world tells us to seek first marriage, a career, or whatever the next item is on our List, but God says we are to place him and his agenda as the priority of our lives—trusting him to take care of the rest.

> **God says we are to place him and his agenda as the priority of our lives—trusting him to take care of the rest.**

So, what exactly does it mean to "seek *first* the kingdom of God"? I was pondering this question recently while at the lake with some friends after church. After a long day of waterskiing, we relaxed on the boat, watching a beautiful sunset. Since the group was in a reflective mood, I threw out this question to see what response I would get. The general consensus from this group (all of whom love God, serve God, and are on fire for his purposes) was that *seeking first the kingdom means passionately pursuing our relationship with Jesus Christ and passionately pursuing* his *agenda instead of our own.*

I'm a big fan of that definition. Seeking first means spending our time, our energy, and our resources furthering the priorities and passions of God's heart—living by his agenda and not our own. Instead of chasing after a guy, a career, or the latest trends, God's desire is that we pour our lives into his kingdom agenda.

Citizen: Kingdom of God

Once we enter a relationship with God through his Son, Jesus Christ, we become citizens of God's kingdom. Colossians 1:13 states that at the point of our salvation, "He [God the Father] has rescued us from the domain of darkness and transferred us into the kingdom of the Son He loves." No longer are we captive to Satan and his agenda of sin, selfishness, and destruction; we are now children of God and our citizenship is in *his* kingdom.

I must press pause on all this deep theology for a second and offer up an illustration to help us understand the significance of this truth. I love to travel, especially internationally. My bags are always packed for some new destination. I often joke with my married friends, "You have babies and I have luggage." My passport is filled with stamps from countries all over the world. While I've eaten, slept, shopped, washed laundry, and driven cars in many different countries, the fact is that I am a citizen of the United States of America. My body may have occupied space in Paris or Prague for a few weeks, but my true residence is Houston, Texas, USA.

I belabor this point to explain the nature of citizenship. No longer are we citizens of this world (even though our bodies temporarily occupy space here). Our true citizenship is in the kingdom of God—the realm in which God rules and reigns as well as where his agenda is priority.

Now as citizens of the kingdom of God, God's agenda becomes our agenda. No longer do we live by the world's agenda that says, "Seek first the kingdom of self," which prioritizes glorifying our own name, pursuing our own happiness, and chasing after the empty trinkets that can never fulfill us. No, as citizens of God's kingdom, we now pledge allegiance to One—King Jesus—and we find our truest joy and purpose in glorifying him and pursuing his agenda.

Jesus teaches us what pursuing the kingdom agenda above all else looks like. His teaching centered on proclaiming it. He compared the kingdom to a pearl of great price. The man in the parable sold all that he owned to purchase this pearl (Matt. 13:45–46). He believed in its value and considered it worth the sacrifice of giving up everything to pursue. Truly, Jesus modeled this verse for us by giving up everything for the kingdom—even his own life.

The fundamental truth of life is this: We are created by God and for God. Anything, and I mean *anything*, we place at the center of our lives except him will crumble. If we choose to seek first a husband or career or a perfect body, then we are putting at the center of our lives something unfit to reign there. Anything we devote ourselves to other than him will ultimately disappoint and leave us wanting and searching for another person, experience, or possession. As John Piper writes, "No thing can satisfy the soul. The soul was made to stand in awe of a Person—the only Person worthy of awe."[1] We seek first King Jesus and his kingdom because he is the only one who can sustain the pressure to exist on the throne of our hearts, and in seeking him, we find all that we truly desire.

> If we choose to seek first a husband or career or a perfect body, then we are putting at the center of our lives something unfit to reign there.

Stop. Think about *your* List for a minute. I'm sure many wonderful things are on it, but are they worth your life? Will you really "feel alive" if you check off everything on it? Or will you wake up one day and think, *There's got to be more to life than this?* When we seek first the kingdom of God, we find our purpose, we find our destiny, and we find life as it is meant to be experienced: full, rich, abundant, blessed, and overflowing. Mack Douglas once said, "Dedicate your life to a cause greater than yourself and your life will become a glorious romance and adventure."[2] Trust me, the greatest adventure imaginable is living for the kingdom agenda. There is no purpose higher, no experience grander, and no cause more rewarding.

The Kingdom Agenda

God's agenda becomes *our* agenda when we become citizens of God's kingdom. His agenda is clearly defined in the two "Great" statements in the Bible: the Great Commandment and the Great Commission. Jesus pronounced the Great Commandment when he was under the scrutiny of the religious leaders of his day. As a means of testing Christ, one of them asked him which of the commandments in Scripture was the greatest. Jesus responded by saying:

> "*Love the Lord your God* with all your heart, with all your soul, and with all your mind. This is the greatest and most important commandment. The second is like it: *Love your neighbor* as yourself. All the Law and the Prophets depend on these two commandments." (Matt. 22:37–40, emphasis mine)

Essentially, in this response, Jesus teaches us that love is at the heart of the kingdom agenda. We love God, and out of the overflow of our relationship with him, we love others.

The second part of the kingdom agenda is found in the Great Commission—Jesus's final instruction (or commission) to his disciples before ascending to heaven:

> Jesus came near and said to them, "All authority has been given to Me in heaven and on earth. *Go,* therefore, and *make disciples* of all nations, baptizing them in the name of the Father and of the Son and of the Holy Spirit, teaching them to observe everything

I have commanded you. And remember, I am with you always, to the end of the age." (Matt. 28:18–20, emphasis mine)

Jesus commissions us to take the message of the gospel (the forgiveness and freedom that is found in him) to the world.

- We are Christ's ambassadors.
- We are Christ's messengers.
- We are Christ's representatives on earth.

In summary, the kingdom agenda is this: we love God and we love others. The greatest way to express love is to share Jesus Christ with someone. Think about it: We are to care about where others will spend eternity. Therefore, the agenda of our lives is *to know Jesus and to make him known*!

How do we make Jesus known to the world today? How do we fulfill the kingdom agenda in our lives? We discover our God niche! Each of us is equipped with spiritual gifts, natural abilities, passions, and experiences: God's unique niche that we were designed to fill in advancing his kingdom agenda.

Discover Your Niche!

The Bible says, "We are God's workmanship, created in Christ Jesus to do good works" (Eph. 2:10 NIV). In *The Purpose Driven Life*, author Rick Warren describes our niche as a "custom combination of capabilities" that God equips each of us with. Warren explains how to discover your personal niche in God's kingdom by using the acronym S.H.A.P.E.

> **Spiritual Gifts**—God gives every believer spiritual gifts to use in ministry.
>
> **Heart**—God has given each of us a unique emotional "heartbeat" that races when we think about subjects, activities, or circumstances that interest us. We instinctively care about some things and not about others. These are clues to where you should be serving (your niche).
>
> **Abilities**—All of our abilities come from God and every ability can be used for his glory!
>
> **Personality**—Your personality will affect how and where you use your spiritual gifts and abilities. God made you to be you—not someone else!
>
> **Experience**—You have been shaped by your experiences in life. God allowed them for the purpose of molding you.[3]

I'll never forget discovering my God niche. I'd been a follower of Jesus Christ for a few years when my pastor called and asked if I would consider teaching a new Bible study class for single adults. I was extremely hesitant at first. Wow, is that an understatement. Honestly, I did not know that teaching was one of my spiritual gifts, and I was so filled with the fear of failure that I almost said no. I recall sitting with my mentor and saying, "They must be crazy. I don't know the first thing about teaching. All I know is that I love Jesus!" Thankfully, I overcame my fears and heeded my church's call to serve.

I must have studied forty hours to teach that first thirty-minute lesson. I loved the preparation time of researching the history of the text; I was blown away by the amazing things God revealed to me when I took the time to really study his Word; and I experienced a whole new level of prayer when approaching God for his strength in my weakness.

Then the big day arrived . . .

I taught my first Bible study lesson. Boy, was I nervous. But I'll never forget walking away that morning and thinking, "This is why I was born." I knew that God had prepared me to serve him in this way. Never in my life had I felt more alive. Never in my life had I felt more on purpose. Never in my life had I felt the power of God working through me.

Girls, I was hooked.

That very first teaching experience opened the door for me to discover my unique God niche. Trust me when I tell you that I was not a great public speaker, nor did I have the best teaching outline, but I knew I was in the center of God's will and doing exactly what he would have me do. In the years since that first lesson, I've grown in my gifting through study, trial and error, learning from other teachers, and allowing God to shape and mold me.

The coolest thing is that I'm still in the niche-discovery process. I've discovered more and more how specifically I am wired to serve

God's kingdom—my niche has become more defined over time. If you had told me ten years ago that today I would be writing books for women, I would have said, "Whatever! Me? A writer? *Puleeeease!*" But all along the way, God shaped me to become the woman I am today.

I had served as a Bible teacher at my church for several years when God placed on my heart the desire to reach non-Christian women through a culturally relevant outreach event. He gave me this crazy idea of using the TV series *Sex and the City* as a means of sharing my story with women and teaching them about the love of Jesus and his truth that set me free. Little did I know where God would take that first event.

My church hosted this event for single women, and we saw hundreds come to know Jesus Christ. I was blown away at how God redeemed my sinful past as a means of bringing other women into the kingdom. That is when I learned more specifically that my niche was not just teaching the Bible but also evangelism (telling others about Jesus) by sharing my testimony. God used that first evangelistic event as the catalyst for me to write my first book, *Sex and the City Uncovered*. After that book was published, God then opened the doors for me to take the same evangelistic event to women across the nation.

Let me just say that for me there is nothing, absolutely nothing, like witnessing someone place her faith in Jesus and find hope, life, and healing in him. Nothing in this world compares to the thrill of being on the front lines of God's kingdom work and introducing women to Jesus Christ.

Today, those two spiritual gifts (teaching and evangelism) compose most of what I do through Redeemed Girl Ministries. I can look back on my life and see God's hand moving and working in every detail to create in me the skills, talents, passions, and gifts I would need to serve him. All along the way God was forming me for his kingdom agenda and using my past experiences, trials, and pain so that I could reach other women with his truth and grace.

Wow, Jesus is so cool.

Let me give you a bit of advice. It's the same advice I give to any girl who asks me the "now" question. Discover your God niche and pour out your life for the kingdom agenda. I guarantee you this: Life will never be boring. How do you do this? First, embrace your season, and second, pray specifically for God to use you in his kingdom.

Embrace the Season

Singleness is a beautiful season to serve God. The fact of the matter is, single girls have a luxury that we often take for granted . . . time. Spend just a day with a woman with children and you'll know what I'm saying is oh-so-true. Between bathing babies, feeding babies, changing babies, cooking dinner, washing laundry, and buying groceries . . . there is a massive shortage of free time.

One thing I've learned as a single girl is that I have a precious gift. This gift is time. Time to travel. Time to learn. Time to serve.

Time to build relationships. Time to study God's Word. Time . . . time . . . time . . . The *single* season is most beautiful when our perspective changes from viewing it as a vacancy to viewing it as an opportunity.

So many women I know look at their lives and see a vacancy: a missing husband, a missing home, and missing children. But I've learned that the single season is beautiful when we instead learn to use it as an opportunity. Opportunity is the operative word here. Here's the thing we must understand: Our perspective on our lives is the very thing that determines our emotional response. If I choose to look at my life and see it as unfulfilled, unimportant, or insignificant, then I'm going to naturally feel disappointed, dissatisfied, and frustrated. But if I choose to look at my life through the lens of God's perfect timing and sovereign plan, then I can embrace the season as an *opportunity* to enjoy instead of a season of suffering.

Embrace your season as an opportunity to discover your God niche.

Look, yours may not mean full-time professional ministry. Thankfully, he has a different plan for each of us, and he wants to use you (with your specific passions and gifts) to advance his kingdom.

I have friends who are doctors, teachers, artists, dancers, singers, and lawyers. Each of them has different spiritual gifts and

> The single season is most beautiful when our perspective changes from viewing it as a vacancy to viewing it as an opportunity.

different passions. Some love serving the poor while others love the arts. Their God niche is different from my own, yet just as important and just as relevant. I like to think of God as this amazing artist who uses a variety of colors and textures in his creation. If we all had the same gifts and talents, then life would be very boring, and that is not how God "rolls."

What's the first step in discovering your niche? Serve! Serve! Serve! You've got the time. Stop making excuses. Find out the needs in your local church and volunteer. Perhaps you will teach second-grade Sunday school or write songs for the worship service, but you'll never know your niche until you step out and try something. Along the way you'll discover your spiritual gifts and the area of ministry that makes you feel "alive."

> **You'll never know your niche until you step out and try something.**

Big Prayers

The summer before I began Redeemed Girl Ministries, I spent a month in England studying at Oxford University with my seminary's master's program. That month was an intense time of learning God's Word and being challenged by professors to pursue God's call on my life. A course about the great revival movements of the church absolutely rocked my world. Something in my soul burned as my professor told stories of the great men and women of the faith God used to advance his kingdom. I recall sitting on the edge of my seat and listening to stories about George Whitefield,

D. L. Moody, and Elisabeth Elliot. Oh, my heart longed to be used by God as they were.

One story I loved was about Moody. One time Moody heard someone say, "The world has yet to see what God can do with a man whose heart is completely devoted to him." Moody's response was, "Lord, I want to be that man." Truly, God used him in extraordinary ways. Before radio or TV, Moody led nearly a million people to faith in Jesus Christ. That's what I call living for the kingdom agenda! On hearing about Moody's life, I thought, "Lord, I want to be that *girl*!"

The small spark for God's kingdom purposes that burned in my heart was now a roaring flame. I, too, wanted God to use my life—all of me—for his kingdom agenda. I spent many hours that summer walking through the parks and streets of Oxford, all the while praying, *God use me. Please give me a vision of the purpose you have for me. Open my eyes to where you want me to go and what you want me to do.* I knew I would never again be content unless I was living out his kingdom purpose for my life.

That summer abroad in Oxford was transformational. Not only did God broaden my perspective and burn in my heart a renewed passion for kingdom work, but he also spoke to me—clearly spoke to me in response to my prayer—concerning my kingdom niche.

On my way home, back to Texas, I sat in London's Gatwick airport awaiting my flight. While there I found a coffee shop and sat reading my Bible. Soon, my quiet time was interrupted with two college girls who sat down and asked me a strange question. "Are you studying the Bible?" they began. "Yes," I replied, half expecting an insult. "Will you please teach us?" they asked expectantly.

Obviously I was surprised by their request. It isn't often that I'm approached by strangers, much less by strangers who actually *want* me to share with them God's Word. But, you see, these girls were curious. They'd spent their summer traveling Europe and seeing the amazing cathedrals and art devoted to Christ over the centuries, but they didn't really know anything about Jesus. They were curious to learn about this Jesus who had affected so much of European history and art. When they saw me reading the Bible, they thought I could help answer their questions.

Girls, I simply have goose bumps as I share with you this moment—this divine appointment when God opened my eyes to see the young women he was calling me to reach. I sat with these girls for nearly an hour and together we looked at the Bible and talked about Jesus. My heart was filled with joy and excitement as I shared with them Christ's love and his mission to redeem humanity.

At the end of our talk, when it was time for us to go catch our flights, I walked away and sensed the Lord say, "Go, *they* are your mission field." That moment in the airport shaped my kingdom agenda. Looking back, I realize that day God called me specifically to reach college women—placing in my heart a passion for them to know Jesus and his redeeming grace.

Of course, God would send me back to minister to that particular age group since I knew firsthand the pain and struggles they experience. My college years were when I was lost, hurt, and in desperate need of the love of God—the time in my own life when I fell for the lies of this world and experienced tremendous brokenness and shame. God was redeeming every aspect of my past, my experiences, and my story to be used for his glory! My God

> My God niche is a compilation of my gifts, experiences, failures, abilities, and passions.

niche is a compilation of my gifts, experiences, failures, abilities, and passions.

What about you? What do you love? What have you experienced in your story that God wants to use in his kingdom? What gifts, experiences, failures, abilities, and passions do you have that can be used for his agenda? Discovering your God niche is the secret to experiencing the beauty of your *single* season.

These Things

Friends, let me tell you the most amazing thing: As I've answered the kingdom call, I've never felt more blessed nor enjoyed my life more. Everyday I'm learning just how true Christ's promise to us is. When he says to "seek first" the kingdom, he adds to this command a promise: that all "these things" will be added to us.

What does Jesus mean by "these things"? I believe that Jesus is referring to the things in life that we desire and long for. You know—the stuff on our List. Now wait a minute. Before you think that I am saying that the List will be delivered to you exactly as you wrote it, if you just do a few godly things first, I want to clarify. I believe that God wants us to believe that by delighting in him, we will find the desires of our hearts (Ps. 37:4, author's paraphrase). Personally, as I've learned to live for the kingdom agenda instead of my own agenda, I've found that God has met desires of my heart that I didn't even know existed. He knows me far better than I know myself. He has the best prepared for me; all he wants from me is to simply trust him.

Girls, take my advice. Seek first the kingdom and let God take care of the List.

> *Break my heart for what breaks Yours.*
> *Everything I am for Your kingdom cause.*
> *As I walk from earth into eternity.*
>
> —Brooke Fraser

Dance

To make your season
beautiful, become a girl
who dances with God.

Dance is the hidden language of the soul.
—MARTHA GRAHAM

The Dance

From the moment he takes her hand the dance begins. The connection is made. Perfect timing. Perfect balance. Perfect rhythm. Step by step the couple swirls across the floor. A vision of fluidity, of poise, of promise. Others watch, barely breathing. He knows her—her pace, her strengths, her weaknesses. He knows when to spin her out and when to pull her toward him. He takes the lead, a strong partner; she is secure in his arms, free to twirl, to dip, and to sway.

She abandons herself to the security of his arms. Lifting her, holding her, releasing her, steadying her, he balances her as she spins across the dance floor. Lights shimmer across the dancers, sashaying in and out of the shadows. They sparkle, graceful, gliding as if on ice. He leads. She follows. She mirrors every step he makes. She is resplendent, aglow with the rhythm of her dance. Chiffon billows around her, clouds of color, an ethereal blur of beauty, gliding effortlessly as he leads, and she follows surrendered to the cadence he has set.

Oneness.

Surrender.

Leading and responding.

Years ago the Lord gave me this image of a couple waltzing to symbolize how a relationship with him was meant to be experienced—not a religion of rigid rules but a beautiful, fluid dance, one where he leads and I follow. His timing. His steps. His music.

When the Lord began teaching me about *his List,* he brought this picture to memory as a reminder that the single season is a beautiful time to learn this dance. Singleness is a time, unlike any other, when a woman can wholeheartedly pursue her relationship with Jesus. She can know him in ways that she cannot if or when she is married.

> Singleness is a time, unlike any other, when a woman can wholeheartedly pursue her relationship with Jesus.

It really is not a shock that the Lord used this illustration with me, for you see, I LOVE TO DANCE! As a little girl, I faithfully watched *American Bandstand* on Saturday mornings. Donning my leg warmers and a kickin' side ponytail, I mimicked the dance moves I watched on TV. Throughout grade school, I took the required tap, ballet, and jazz classes. I adored my pink tutus and the thrill of a dance recital in a cafetorium (definition: school cafeteria that doubles as a performance hall). Sadly, my Broadway dream ended with the whopping ten inches I grew in eighth grade—leaving me five feet eleven and what some would call "a tiny bit awkward." Yet, it was not until my high school days that I discovered my absolute favorite dance of all—the Texas two-step.

I need you to imagine the movie *Footloose* for a minute. (You know, Kevin Bacon and Sarah Jessica Parker circa 1984. Greatest sound track ever, I might add. Am I right or am I right?) Girls, I loved *Footloose* for more than just the music and excellent '80s fashion. I loved it because, well, I lived it. Take one small Texas town, mix in one rebellious young woman, add George Strait playing on the jukebox, and my big-blonde-Texas hair spinning across the dance floor, and, well, you have a pretty good picture of my teenage years. Sure, this activity required sneaking out of my parents' house, crossing the county line, and using a fake ID to get into a honky-tonk called Cotton Eye Joes. (I couldn't make this up if I tried.) There, in my own version of the '80s classic, I learned how to dance—the waltz, the West Coast swing, the polka, and of course, the Texas two-step.

Although I was far from spiritual back then, learning this type of dancing was in many ways a spiritual training ground. I'm still amazed how God redeems everything for his glory! Dancing taught me scores of lessons that apply directly to my relationship with Jesus.

Rule 1—The Name of the Dance Is Surrender

Here's a dance fact that every girl needs to know: When two people dance, only one person can lead. If both try, there's that

> When two people dance, only one person can lead.

inevitable moment of toe-crushing pain, followed by stiff and jerky movements, and a few awkward apologies. I should know. Oh, the memories! I can recall numerous times when some cute cowboy would ask me to dance, and it would only take a short eight count for me to begin trying to set the pace. If my partner was a bad dancer or lacked rhythm, I got away with it, but if the guy knew how to dance, he'd stop in the middle of the dance floor, look me square in the eye, and say, "How 'bout you let *me* lead, darlin'?" I learned my lesson. For a dance to be fluid and beautiful, one must surrender to the lead of the other.

Surrender is a tough word, but it's essential to the Christian life and absolutely vital for making any season of life beautiful. The attitude of surrender says, "You are God and I am not." It declares, "I'm not in control here." Surrender is choosing to let go and let God lead . . . or as Carrie Underwood would sing, "Jesus, take the wheel." (Sorry, but I couldn't stop myself.) Whatever metaphor you choose, they all speak the same language—yielding, submitting, abandoning, and relinquishing control.

When dancing with Jesus, what we surrender is our *will*. The human will is our capacity to choose or make decisions. Every human being has a will, and we all make choices. Just today I decided to wash my car, shop for groceries, read the Bible, and call a few friends. I also chose to eat mac and cheese *instead* of a salad. I chose *not* to make my bed. And, I chose to check Facebook when I should have been writing.

We also choose (with our will) whether we will submit to God's plan and purpose for us or insist on trying to control our own lives. Here's the interesting thing about God: He doesn't override our free will. He did not create us like robots that mechanically follow his lead. No, we are human beings, made in his image with the capacity to choose; therefore, following Jesus is a choice. We choose to obey. We choose to respond to his voice. We choose to let him lead us in the way he would have us go.

Surrender is our response to what God has done in rescuing us from our sin. As the Bible says, "Dear brothers and sisters, I plead with you to give your bodies to God because of all he has done for you. Let them be a living and holy sacrifice—the kind he will find acceptable. This is truly the way to worship him" (Rom. 12:1 NLT). I hope you noticed the connection made in this verse. We willingly hand over direction of our lives to God because of all that he has done for us. This response is best illustrated in a story that I originally shared in my book *Sex and the City Uncovered*.

> I heard a story one time about Abraham Lincoln. Legend has it he attended a slave auction years before he became President of the United States. Lincoln watched from a distance as one by one men and women were brought before the crowd to be auctioned to the highest bidder. After watching in disgust for a while he turned to go when he saw a young woman brought to the platform to be sold. Her eyes gleamed with anger and her chin jutted out with defiance.
>
> Her asking price would be high because she was perfect for work on a plantation. The auctioneer started the bidding and many hands went up. One hand in particular was that of Abraham Lincoln, himself. And he kept raising his hand that day until he bought her.
>
> Once the deal was done and she belonged to him, Lincoln walked up to her and said the unthinkable,

"you are free." Her face bore the same look of anger and defiance that she wore as her worth had been determined on that platform. Glaring at him she spat out, "free for what?" Lincoln said, "you are free. Free to go. I bought you in order to set you free." As the truth settled into her heart, the expression upon her face softened and with love overflowing, she said, "then I'm going with you."[1]

The woman in this story chose to follow the one who set her free. Our response to Christ is the same . . . we choose to follow him because of the amazing gift of freedom he purchased for us with his redeeming death on the cross.

I wish I could tell you that the act of surrender is a one-time occurrence and with the flip of a switch, we instantly fall in line with Christ's steps. Not so. With every beat of the music, we choose to lead or to follow. As Rick Warren noted in *The Purpose Driven Life*, "There is a moment of surrender, and there is the practice of surrender, which is moment-by-moment and lifelong."[2] We decide every day and every moment whether or not we will follow the lead of Jesus.

> **We decide every day and every moment whether or not we will follow the lead of Jesus.**

When I became a Christian, I faced a decision: Will I allow Jesus to lead, or will I continue trying to determine the steps? Will I lay down my agenda, my ways, and my plans and allow the Lord to direct me, or will I sit on the sidelines, watching others dance while I sulk and insist on having my way? Through a series of circumstances, God brought me to a place where I said, "I want your will. I want you to lead, not me." Reflecting on that time, I realize that I came face-to-face with my own humanity. I couldn't control my life or the events surrounding it. I would either surrender my will to the God who spoke this world into existence and who sustains it by his awesome power, or I would foolishly try to control my own life and find myself frustrated day in and day out by my own inability to rule the universe. Friends, this was by far the best decision I've ever made, and the most logical, I might add.

When we surrender our lives to Jesus, we are saying "God, I desire your will. I want what you want. I choose to go where you lead." This surrender is tested at every new turn on the dance floor. Sometimes the Lord dips us when we expect him to turn us, and in that moment we must choose—his will or mine?

Mary, a Portrait of Surrender

"May it be done to me according to your word" (Luke 1:38). These words were the simple response of a simple girl to do the will of her God—painting for us a portrait of complete surrender. Mary was just an ordinary young Jewish woman betrothed to a man named Joseph when the angel Gabriel visited her with the surprising news that she would be the mother of the Savior of the world. Centuries of anticipation. Hundreds of prophecies. One girl. One message. One choice—her will or God's will? The nation of Israel had waited for the promised Messiah, and shockingly God revealed his redemptive plan to a teenage girl who would miraculously bear his Son.

On one hand, this news was thrilling, but on the other hand, the cost of surrender for Mary was extremely high. In Mary's Jewish culture, a woman became engaged in a public ceremony that pledged her to her future husband. They remained betrothed for a period of time, sometimes a year, before being married as husband and wife. In those days, it was legal for any woman found pregnant out of wedlock to be stoned to death. Even if Joseph pardoned her, given the societal mores of the time, she fully expected that she would be disgraced, that her fiancée (who knew *he* wasn't the father) would abandon her, and that she probably would never marry.

I just wonder, did Mary have a List? Of course she did. What woman, engaged to be married, doesn't have a List? I'm just guessing, but something tells me Mary's List may have gone a little something like this:

1. Joseph will ask my father for my hand in marriage and then he will propose. (Check. Check.)
2. Then we will be engaged! Oh, the bliss. I will have so much work to do preparing for the big wedding. Find a dress. Pick my bridesmaids. Order the baklava cake. (Check. Check. Check!)
3. Marriage! Joseph and I will officially become husband and wife!

4. Following a whirlwind honeymoon around the Sea of Galilee, we will settle down in a little bungalow in North Nazareth, surrounded by family and friends.

5. Joseph will open a nice carpentry business while I create a warm and loving home for the family we plan to have one day. Our kids will play with the neighbors, we will host family reunions, and the big event of our lives will be the yearly pilgrimage to Jerusalem for Passover.

Such a nice plan, don't ya think? Well, as we know, life didn't go according to Mary's plan. Somewhere between her second and third goals, Mary was visited by the angel Gabriel. Instead of her List, Mary would face the humiliation of a public scandal; watch in bewilderment as a chorus of angels and wise men worshipped at the birth of her son; flee with her husband and son to Egypt to escape a jealous king's wrath; watch in wonder as the incarnate One learned to crawl, walk, talk, and read; and experience the excruciating pain of watching the son she loved dearly take up a cross and die for the sins of the world.

We can try to imagine ourselves in Mary's dance shoes, but I don't expect we can ever truly grasp the gravity of her decision to exchange her List for God's List. Mary knew there would be challenges . . . big ones! But rather than focusing on the size of her problems, she chose to trust in the size of her God. She focused on his purpose for her life rather than her own. Her humble reply said it all, "I am the Lord's servant. . . . May it be to me as you have said" (Luke 1:38 NIV).

Mary danced.

Trusting God with her life, she said yes to his will. While Mary's dance was a difficult one, requiring a level of surrender few of us can imagine, the outcome of her surrender was nothing less than magnificent—the salvation of the world.

Mary proved to be a brilliant instructor because of her trust in God. Mary did not understand many things that happened in her life, but she knew God and trusted him. Sure, she had to lay down her List for a far higher calling, but she did so because she believed God. She knew that he was faithful, loving, and good. She knew he was true to his word. Because of her faith, she trusted him even when the plan did not make sense. She believed him when her logic told her to do otherwise. She danced with God even when the dance chosen for her tested her trust in him.

> So often we think we need to take back control because we don't really trust that God is able to lead our lives the way we think they should go.

So often, many of us refuse to surrender because of our lack of trust. The issue is one of faith. Do we really believe God can handle the details and circumstances of our lives? So often we think we need to take back control because we don't really trust that God is able to lead our lives the way we think they should go.

The ability to trust your dance partner is a huge aspect of surrender. I know this one from experience. I'm not what you would call petite. I'm a tall girl . . . OK, so I'm really, really tall. So, when dancing with a guy who knows how to dance (i.e., lift, spin, dip, etc.), I always face that moment when I ask myself, "Is this guy strong enough to lift me?" Body-image issues aside, this is a scary place for a girl. What if he lifts me over his head and then drops me flat on the ground? What if he can't carry me? Besides the embarrassment, it could really hurt!

When dancing with God, we can relax in his arms and trust in his ability to lift, swing, guide, and hold us up. We are never too heavy. We are never too much trouble. Friends, I have tough questions for you: Do you trust God? Do you trust him enough to surrender your plans, your List, your desires? Do you believe he is able to lead and guide you? Do you want to dance? Better yet, do you want to let him lead?

Early on in Mary's dance she came to this decision. Facing the choice of whether to lead or to follow, she chose the latter, and as a result of her surrender, her heart was filled with joy. The following is a portion of Mary's song, also known as the Magnificat. Here she praised God for his plan, his purposes, his power, and his presence in her life . . . rejoicing in the beauty of the dance!

> "My soul glorifies the Lord and my spirit rejoices in God my Savior, for he has been mindful of the humble state of his servant. From now on all generations will call me blessed, for the Mighty One has done great things for me—holy is his name." (Luke 1:46–49 NIV)

Rule 2—The Name of the Step Is Love

Something I do quite a bit in my profession is answer questions. After I speak at a women's conference or girls' event, there is typically a time set aside for Q&A. Since I'm often speaking to new Christians, one question frequently asked of me is this: How does God want me to live now that I'm a follower of Jesus? My answer is simple: Love God and love others.

Friends, all of God's law is summed up in one word—love. Take the Ten Commandments for instance. The first five deal with our relationship with God and are rooted in loving him, his name, and his glory above all else. The second five deal with our relationships with others. Love doesn't steal. Love doesn't lie. Love doesn't gossip. Love doesn't murder. Essentially, dancing with God is also a two-step . . . love God, love others.

If I love Jesus, then I love following Jesus.

Pondering the beauty of the dance, I thought of how simple the steps are to follow. God does not require a complicated technique of hard-to-follow movements. No, when we dance with Jesus, we always know if we are "in step" or not. Jesus never leads us to step in a way that does not love; his movements are glorifying to our heavenly Father and the perfect picture of grace.

One thing I ask of God every day is this: *Give me a heart to love you more than anything else in this world.* I've learned this is the secret to the dance. If I love Jesus, then I love following Jesus. I delight in his will and in his ways. When my life is focused on loving Jesus, then his love fills my heart and naturally and grace-fully overflows to others, thus fulfilling the Great Commandment. The following Scripture perfectly encapsulates this movement of loving God and loving others:

> Dear friends, let us *love one another*, because *love is from God,* and *everyone who loves has been born of God* and knows God. The one who does not love does not know God, because *God is love.* God's love was revealed among us in this way: God sent His One and Only Son into the world so that we might live through Him. Love consists in this: not that we loved God, but that He loved us and sent His Son to be the propitiation for our sins. Dear friends, *if God loved us in this way, we also must love one another.* No one has ever seen God. *If we love one another, God remains in us and His love is perfected in us.* (1 John 4:7–12, emphasis mine)

Two Become One

Last night I decided I needed to do a little "research." A few friends invited me to go country and western dancing, so I dusted off my boots and gave it a whirl. Let me just echo the timeless words from the movie *Girls Just Wanna Have Fun: I love to dance!* I'd almost forgotten the thrill of (a) being asked to dance, (b) twirl-ing around a dance floor with a guy who knows what he's doing, and (c) that moment of perfect unity when two dance as one.

Oneness is the goal of the dance. When a girl surrenders to her partner, trusts his leadership, knows the steps, and recognizes his direction, then the couple moves together as one to the music. Oneness is also a picture of our relationship with God. The Bible says, "But he who unites himself with the Lord is one with him in spirit" (1 Cor. 6:17 NIV). Jesus explained this union and prayed for our oneness with him the night before his crucifixion:

> "I am praying not only for these disciples but also for all who will ever believe in me through their message. I pray that they will all be *one,* just as *you and I are one*—as you are in me, Father, and I am in you. And may they be in us so that the world will believe you sent me.
>
> "I have given them the glory you gave me, so they may be one as we are one. I am in them and you are in me. May they experience such *perfect unity* that the world will know that you sent me and that *you love them as much as you love me.* Father, I want these whom you have given me to be with me where I am. Then they can see all the glory you gave me because you loved me even before the world began!" (John 17:20–24 NLT, emphasis mine)

When we dance with Jesus, his thoughts become our thoughts, his desires become our desires, and his ways become our ways.

Any woman in love knows what I'm talking about. When you love someone you desire to please that person. Granted, a woman's passion for watching *Monday Night Football* may fade after a few months of courtship, but as a general rule when we love a person, we love what he loves. What I've noticed in my own life over the years is this: The more I've fallen in love with Jesus, the more I long for his will and his purpose in my life. The more we become one, the more I want what he wants and love what he loves.

A woman named Frances Ridley Havergal danced with Jesus. Havergal is best known for her poetry that expressed how passionately she loved her Lord. One of her poems, written in 1874, became the classic hymn "Take My Life and Let It Be." Since oneness with Jesus is a chief desire of my heart, I often use this poem in my quiet time as a prayer of devotion to the Lord.

> Take my life, and let it be
> Consecrated, Lord, to Thee.
> Take my moments and my days;
> Let them flow in ceaseless praise.
>
> Take my hands, and let them move
> At the impulse of Thy love.
> Take my feet, and let them be
> Swift and beautiful for Thee.
>
> Take my voice, and let me sing,
> Always, only, for my King.
> Take my lips, and let them be
> Filled with messages from Thee.

Take my silver and my gold;
Not a mite would I withhold.
Take my intellect, and use
Every power as Thou shalt choose.

Take my will, and make it Thine;
It shall be no longer mine.
Take my heart, it is Thine own;
It shall be Thy royal throne.

Take my love; my Lord, I pour
At Thy feet its treasure-store.
Take myself, and I will be
Ever, only, all for Thee.

In these words Havergal perfectly expressed the surrender, trust, love, and oneness that occur when a woman dances with Jesus. Her will is God's will. Her days are God's days. Her gifts are God's gifts. Her love is God's love.

She moves as one with her Lord.

She is surrendered to his will.

She loves him and his love flows from her life.

She is abandoned to the beauty of the dance.

The Beauty of the Dance

I still can't get over the fact that *he, Jesus,* asked *me* to dance. The God of the universe picked me! Let me just confess, I was a very unlikely candidate. The day he called my name and took my hand, I was a mess. Yet, Jesus looked at me and saw something I never could see in myself—he saw a girl created to twirl.

My dance with Jesus began when I was twenty-four years old. Back then, I didn't know the meaning of surrender nor did I know the steps of love, but I did know that Jesus had captured my heart and he was inviting me to join him on the dance floor.

I still get butterflies writing these words!

A few years have gone by since he first took my hand in his and the music began to play. Years filled with incredible joy and some with tremendous pain, but one thing I know for sure is this: I've danced!

> **Jesus looked at me and saw something I never could see in myself—he saw a girl created to twirl.**

The season since that dreadful birthday has been hands-down one of the most thrilling of my entire life. It was then (when God called me to exchange my List for his) that God asked me to let him lead our dance in what was both unexpected and unknown. My only responsibility was to hold on tight and spin. Today, the tempo is fast and I'm hanging on as Jesus and I twirl across the dance floor.

I simply had no idea how much fun it would be for God to say no to my List.

- I did not get married before age twenty-five.
- I did not become a mom before age thirty.
- I did not get my plan, my agenda, or my List.

And friends, about all I can say to that is this: **PRAISE GOD FROM WHOM ALL BLESSINGS FLOW!**

You know what I got instead of my List? I GOT LIFE! That's right. Jesus did not lie. He *did* come that we would experience life abundantly (John 10:10). I'm the first to confess that letting go of my List was hard. Oh, let me rephrase that; it was more like a death. I had such a tight grip on that sucker that I was getting paper cuts. Honestly, I thought I knew *far* better than God what my life was supposed to look like. Funny thing is, last time I checked, I am not the all-knowing, sovereign, Creator of the world.

So, in surrendering my will to God's will, I am blessed beyond words by the dance he's chosen for me. I've enjoyed experiences (ministry, travel, education) that I never could have imagined had God given me "my way." I've formed precious relationships that I would have missed out on had "my plan" been realized. Girlfriends, I hope you'll dance, trusting your desires and longings to the one who knows your heart far better than you do.

Now that I think about it, that is the beauty of the dance. When we dance with Jesus, we are in the arms of the one who knows our hearts, for he fashioned our hearts. He knows our deepest desires, for he placed them there. He knows what will truly bring us the greatest joy, for we were created by him.

The beauty of the dance is best summarized in one of my all-time favorite Scriptures, which says, "Trust in the LORD with all your heart and lean not on your own understanding; in all your ways acknowledge him, and he will make your paths straight"

(Prov. 3:5–6 NIV). This verse reminds me that when dancing with Jesus, I can trust the direction he leads me.

Girls, for the record, I flat out love my single season.

No regrets.

Not one.

I can't believe I'm saying this, but I'm staring my next birthday square in the eyes and I've never been happier. If you would have asked me a decade ago how I would have felt in this moment, I would have told you to call 9-1-1, but I can honestly say, God *does* make *everything* beautiful in its time!

> *I've learned the safest place
> in the world is in the center
> of the will of God.*
>
> —Corrie ten Boom

CONCLUSION

The Choice

Delight yourself in the LORD and he will
give you the desires of your heart.
—PSALM 37:4 NIV

The Bottom Line

So now what? I'll be honest, I still have desires, but I have a different mind-set than I did a few years ago. Every day I choose to joyfully embrace the season of life that God has ordained for me as an opportunity to glorify him. I choose to exchange my List for his List—to shine for his glory, pursue his beauty, hope in him, seek first his kingdom, and dance! You wanna know why? I make this choice because nothing in the world compares with living by God's List.

Here's the bottom line: I want to make this exchange because I've realized that in doing so, I have overwhelming joy and I have peace. Hear me when I tell you that I was flat-out miserable before, and my lack of trust and surrender were keeping me from experiencing the blessings God has for me *now*. I've learned that every one of God's promises are true; it is my choice to believe them.

I believe "everything is beautiful in its time" (Eccles. 3:11 NIV).

I believe if I "delight myself in the Lord, he will give me the desires of my heart" (Ps. 37:4, author paraphrase).

I believe "Every good and perfect gift is from above, coming down from the Father of the heavenly lights, who does not change like shifting shadows" (James 1:17 NIV).

I believe "God works all things for the good of those who love Christ Jesus" (Rom. 8:28, author paraphrase).

I believe "God is good and his lovingkindness endures forever!" (Ps. 136:1, author paraphrase).

And . . .

I believe with every fiber of my being that, "No eye has seen, nor ear heard, nor mind conceived what God has prepared for those who love Him" (1 Cor. 2:9 NIV).

The amazing thing is that by believing God's promises I am the one who is blessed. No longer do I wallow in miserable self-pity, envy, and despair. Oh no! I am content in God's sovereign plan and his joy overflows.

This is not being fake and pretending we don't have desires or sappily acting like life is perfect. No, joy is the by-product of choosing to believe God and trust his timing—believing that God ordains each season of our lives for a reason.

This lesson was learned the hard way. Friends, my insistence on having my List was robbing me of the beauty of the season I was in. I was the girl always looking down the road of life, thinking that real joy would be found at some future destination. Never content in the present because I thought happiness was awaiting me at the next rung on the ladder. No more! I now believe God. Everything *is* beautiful in its time. As a result of this belief, I am determined not to look back on this season and ask myself:

- *What if* I had embraced that time as an opportunity to glorify God?
- *What if* I had made the decision to enjoy the single season instead of wishing it away?
- *What if* I had taken advantage of singleness and truly made it something beautiful?

Attitude Adjustment

Today I still find myself in this season called singleness, but with an entirely different attitude. I get it now. I understand that in this God-appointed time I have an incredible opportunity to glorify Jesus in ways I simply cannot when/if I am married. Therefore, I've made the decision to live a no-regrets single life.

And, friends, let me just say, "Wow!" God has blown me away with his List. Looking back, I can now see how bland, boring, and predictable my List really was. You see, God had in store for me a life full of faith-stretching adventures and awe-inspiring opportunities. Living by his List is not the American dream or the scene from a romantic comedy. No, his List is far greater. Truly, this life is epic! The only regret I have is that I didn't embrace his List sooner.

> Living by his List is not the American dream or the scene from a romantic comedy. No, his List is far greater. Truly, this life is epic!

What about you? How can you glorify God in your season? How can you choose today to joyfully embrace your circumstance as an opportunity to make *him* famous? How can you advance his kingdom?

Friends, this attitude is a choice.

P.S. Life is full of choices. Every season of life can be brutal or beautiful—it truly just depends on the attitude we choose. I've discovered a sad fact as I talk to women across the nation. A girl can acquire every single item on her List and still be miserable—and make those around her miserable as well. The secret to life is not in acquiring all of the many items on our teenage agendas. Nope. It is found in *abandoning* ourselves fully to the will of God and choosing to glorify him in any and every situation.

Single or married.

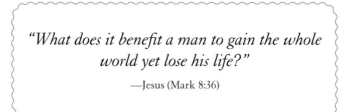

"What does it benefit a man to gain the whole world yet lose his life?"

—Jesus (Mark 8:36)

Small-group Questions

Hey Girls!

I am such a BIG fan of small groups. There is nothing in the world like a group of girls studying God's Word and sharing life together. I know from personal experience that God works mightily in a small group devoted to knowing and loving Jesus and one another.

I pray the following discussion questions will help you and your girlfriends figure out this whole issue of Prince Charming, the Corner Office, and Happily Ever After. And I pray your group will "laugh 'til you cry and cry 'til you laugh" . . . and through it all, fall head over heels in love as you dance with Jesus!

Your friend and sister in Christ,

Marian

P.S. If you are a small-group leader, there is a Leader's Guide just for you available for download at www.redeemedgirl.org.

Introduction: The List

1. Marian describes trying to "boycott her birthday" due to the pain of unmet expectations. Can you relate to the emotions she felt at the time?

2. The List can go by many names, but the premise is the same. Please share with the group what your List would have been at age thirteen.

3. How does your List still influence you today?

4. How did your culture shape and influence your List? Parents? Movies? Books? TV? Education? Celebrities? Friends?

5. Marian says, "My angst wasn't about getting *older* per se—my anguish was more the result of unmet expectations. I always imagined my life would look different by this age." How is your life currently lining up with your List? Is there one thing specifically that brings you anguish?

6. Read Ecclesiastes 3:1–11. God's Word says to us that everything is beautiful in its time. Do you see your season of life as beautiful? Yes or no? Why?

7. Marian dealt with her unmet expectations by talking to God in prayer. Have you talked to God about your List? Why or why not?

The Bible says in 1 Peter 5:7 to cast your cares on God because he cares about you. Take time in your small group to "cast your cares" on God. Talk to him about your unmet expectations and your List.

Number 1: Shine

1. Marian describes many TV shows that depict our fame-seeking culture. Name a few that come to mind which portray man's desire for glory, attention, fame, and praise.
2. How are our Lists shaped by this human desire for glory and fame? (Marriage? Career? Social Status?)
3. Marian writes, "To understand why we were made, we first must recognize the fact that we are, indeed, 'made.' Created. Formed. Designed. Planned. Fashioned. We are not self-existent creatures. We did not create ourselves. We are the purposeful design of one who is the Creator of all things. The Author of life. The holy, awesome, and majestic God of the universe."

   How does the fact that we are created change the way you see the purpose of your life?
4. What does Isaiah 43:6–7 say that our purpose is in life?
5. How does believing this truth challenge our Lists?
6. Read John 10:10. Jesus says that Satan came to steal, kill, and destroy. How has the Enemy sought to kill your joy and destroy your testimony in this season of life?
7. Marian confessed in this chapter that many items on her List were more about her glory than she cared to

admit. Can you confess the same? How can the fairy-tale wedding, perfect job, corner office, social status, and perfect family photo become more about our glory instead of God's glory?

8. On page 24, Marian speaks about the battle raging for glory. How do you see that battle raging in your life?

9. When are you most prone to be a Bridezilla? (Translation: When are you tempted to make life "all about you"?)

10. Think about your calendar and credit card statement. Based on what you see, what are you shining for currently? What are you living to glorify?

11. Why do our hearts resist keeping God at the center of our lives?

12. In this chapter, Marian describes life in the sweet spot. This is living life centered on God's glory. Are there any changes you need to make in order to live for his glory and fame?

13. Pray with your group to have a heart that desires His glory above all else.

Number 2: Hope

1. Marian shares her addiction to infomercials. What is your personal favorite commercial? How are these a great example of hope that sells? When is a time you have bought into someone hocking hope?

2. Read the following excerpt: "I define *hope* as desire with the expectation of fulfillment. The word *expectation* is so huge, for expecting is the activity of hope. When I hope, I choose to place my expectation in the thing I believe will deliver a good and positive outcome."

   What illustrations of hope does Marian use in this chapter?

3. What is a BLD? Share with the group a few examples of big letdowns in your life.

4. If you were to rewrite Psalm 33 (similarly to how Marian did on pages 48–49) what would fill in your blanks?

5. Explain the difference between false hope and real hope.

6. Psalm 33:16–17 describes the false hopes that Israel trusted. What are your false hopes (i.e., the perfect guy, a big bank account, a perfect body, your List)?

7. How do we hope in God?

8. Why is trust in God's love for us essential to placing our hope in him?

9. In this chapter, Marian details a lunch meeting with a friend who confessed a lack of faith in God to deliver the desires of her heart. How have you been tempted to take matters into your own hands instead of waiting on God to deliver your desires?

   What potentially negative consequences can result from this choice?

10. Read the following Scripture together as a group prayer:

    We wait in hope for the LORD;

    he is our help and our shield.

    In him our hearts rejoice,

    for we trust in his holy name.

    May your unfailing love rest upon us, O LORD,

    even as we put our hope in you.

    (Ps. 33:20–22 NIV)

Number 3: Pursue Beauty

1. How does our culture define beauty?
2. How is the pursuit of external beauty reflected in your List?
3. In the opening of this chapter, Marian is honest about her pursuit of external beauty. How can you relate? How have worldly images of beauty influenced you?
4. Marian writes, "The term *plastic* has become synonymous with a girl who's extremely attractive on the outside, yet empty and shallow on the inside—a type of beauty that's literally only skin deep. It seems that as more focus is placed on external beauty, the uglier the heart can become."

    Do you agree or disagree with this statement?

    Marian adds: "My point is that when we are tempted to fixate on our outer beauty only (skin, hair, makeup, outfit, size), the result is that we are focusing exclusively on ourselves. This fight for the perfect look is a losing battle with casualties named kindness, goodness, gentleness, and selflessness."

How does this type of self-focus create a "mean girl"?

5. What can we learn from *Jane Eyre* about true beauty?

6. What is the secret to becoming truly beautiful? (Hint: Abide . . . Behold . . . Become.)

7. How do we reflect the Beautiful One?

8. As a group, commit to daily "beholding the Beautiful One." "Beautiful Time Tips" follows this section. Review the tips together now.

9. What insight did "A Guy's Perspective" give you into this whole issue of beauty?

10. What things in your heart are far from beautiful? Read and apply Psalm 139:23–24. Ask God to show you if there is anything "plastic" that you need to confess (gossip, slander, lying, pride, rude speech, unkind words, bitterness, greed, jealousy, or selfish attitudes).

11. As a group, pray and ask God to make you a woman who radiates the Beautiful One.

Number 4: Seek First

1. Marian writes: "Over the last few years I've encountered hundreds of young women who . . . are twenty-ish, thirty-ish, and dare I say it . . . forty-ish, and still single (or single again) . . . and many are asking the 'now' question.

They do love Jesus, but their List is nowhere to be found; therefore, they are confused, disillusioned, and frankly, feeling a little bit lost. Aside from the loneliness and disappointment, most of them just want to know what they are supposed to do . . . in the meantime. You know, that span of time between graduation and getting hitched."

Can you relate to the "now" question these women are asking?

2. How have you been spending your single season? What have you been doing with your time and freedom?

3. What does it mean to "seek first the kingdom of God"?

4. Read Colossians 1:13 and discuss the significance of citizenship in God's kingdom.

5. What does this world/culture encourage us to seek first?

6. What is the kingdom agenda? Are you currently living for this agenda or your own?

7. What is your God niche? What gifts, talents, abilities, passions, and experiences can you use to further the kingdom of God?

8. It has been said, "Where your greatest gift meets the world's greatest need, that is your calling." How can you begin to use your S.H.A.P.E. for God's glory and kingdom agenda today? How can you take action and begin using your gifts, talents, and abilities in your local church?

9. Marian writes: "One thing I've learned as a single girl is that I have a precious gift. This gift is time. Time to travel.

Time to learn. Time to serve. Time to build relationships. Time to study God's Word. Time . . . time . . . time . . . The *single* season is most beautiful when our perspective changes from viewing it as a vacancy to viewing it as an opportunity."

How does the perspective of time as an "opportunity" instead of "vacancy" change your attitude about your season?

10. What "good things" can get in the way of you accomplishing great things for God's kingdom?

Number 5: Dance

1. Please share with the group your favorite dancing memory. (As I write these questions, my assistant is reenacting a second-grade jazz number to the song "Freak Out!" Good times. I hope your group has as much fun reliving eighth-grade slow dances and dance recitals as we are.)

2. How does dancing illustrate our relationship with God?

3. What is surrender? How do we surrender to God?

4. When you've tried to control your life or "lead the dance," what have been the consequences?

5. What can we learn from Mary's dance? How is she a role model for us today?

6. How do trust and surrender go hand in hand?

7. Marian writes: "One thing I ask of God every day is this: *Give me a heart to love you more than anything else*

in this world. I've learned this is the secret to the dance. If I love Jesus, then I love following Jesus. I delight in his will and in his ways. When my life is focused on loving Jesus, then his love fills my heart and naturally and gracefully overflows to others, thus fulfilling the Great Commandment."

Why is loving Jesus essential to the dance?

8. Discuss the "oneness" found in dancing with Jesus.

9. Marian expresses in this chapter her incredible joy that God did not give her everything on her List. What do you think of her testimony?

10. Do you believe God's plan for your life is better than your plan?

11. Read Psalm 37:3–8; 1 Corinthians 2:9; Isaiah 55:9; and Jeremiah 29:11–13. Take time as a group to pray for hearts that are surrendered to God's plan and to follow where he leads. Read the poem "Take My Life" as a prayer together.

Number 6: The Choice

1. How has your perspective on life changed since reading this book?

2. How are you different today?

3. Is the choice to exchange your List for God's List one that you want to make? Why or why not?

4. Looking back over God's List, which is the most challenging to you? Which excites you the most?

5. How can you make your season beautiful starting today?

6. How can you share your new wisdom and insight with other women who are still struggling without their Lists? Read 2 Corinthians 1:3–4.

Challenge: Encourage a girl you know who is feeling disappointed and discouraged in her season.

Beautiful Time Tips

As we figured out in chapter 3, the secret to true beauty is spending time each day with the Beautiful One (Jesus). The method I use for my daily quiet time is called R.E.A.P. (read, examine, apply, pray).[1] All you need is your Bible, a journal, a quiet place, and an open heart. This method is best used with a Bible reading plan. (A Bible reading plan can be found at www.redeemedgirl.org.)

Read

At the top of a sheet of paper (or in a journal), write the date and leave a space to write the title of your entry later. Pick a Scripture to study either by using a Bible reading plan or by coming up with one on your own. I suggest using a daily Bible reading plan. Prayerfully read the text. Ask God to speak to you from his Word.

Next, spend time reflecting and writing in your journal pages about what you've read.

Examine

Write down the key Scripture (or two) that stuck out to you. For example, if reading John 1:1–14, you may write down verse 14 as your key Scripture.

Write down *what* this Scripture says and *why* it matters.

Write down thoughts on what you've read from the entire section.

Ask the important examination questions as you read the text:

- Who (audience, speaker, subject)?
- What (context, purpose, problem)?
- When (time, duration, season)?
- Where (setting, situation, location)?
- Why (motivation, purpose, intent, lesson, truth)?
- How (call to action, example to follow)?

Apply

How does this text apply to your life, circumstances, and relationship with God?

Write out how you will be different today because of what you have just read.

Respond in your journal to the following questions and anything else that comes to mind.

1.   What do I learn about God (the Father, the Son, and the Spirit) from this Scripture?

2. What do I learn about myself from this Scripture?

3. What commands/instructions should I obey?

4. What truth can I apply to my life?

5. What sin do I need to confess?

6. What error can I avoid?

7. What promises can I claim?

Prayer

Write out a personal prayer based on your time in God's Word.

Acknowledgments

I owe a huge debt of gratitude to so many for their faithful prayers, support, and contributions to *The List*. First, a special appreciation to my "write" hands: Angel Texada and Catherine King. I absolutely adore you girls. Truly, I can't imagine a better creative and editorial team. Thank you for serving God with your amazing gifts.

To the board of directors and prayer team for *Redeemed Girl Ministries*: Anita, Kitty, Tonya, Matt, Jeff, Ryan and Kim, Leti and Chaz, Leigh, Susan, Amy S., Brent S., Jennifer A., Amy and Clint, Manonne, Muriel, Marci, Jodi, Mom and Dad. You guys are the best! I am overwhelmed with thankfulness as I think of the support and prayers you provide. Heaven alone knows the mountains that your prayers have moved!

To Keri Greer for coordinating the Women's Bible Study at Second Baptist and to all the Single Life girls for living the List with me.

To the wonderful team at B&H Publishing. I'm so blessed to work with individuals who passionately love Jesus and who desire for women to know him.

To my home church: Second Baptist Church of Houston. Thank you for allowing me the joy of serving alongside you in God's kingdom.

To my amazing "God-gift" of an assistant, Lauren. I simply can't imagine how I ever did ministry without you. I'm so proud of the woman of God you are and how you live God's List.

To my incredible family—Mom and Dad and the whole Jordan/Pope/Johnson crew: I love you guys so much! Thank you all for your grace, support, prayers, and love. I am one blessed girl!

Finally, to my sweet Jesus—thank you, thank you, thank you for asking me to dance!

About the Author

Have you ever seen a street after a parade? The lonesome scraps and fragments that are left seem dirty, abandoned, and trashed. Run-over. What a shift from the moment before when music trilled, drums beat, people danced, and colors burst through our senses, drawing us closer and closer with the goal to press as closely to the barricade as humanly possible. What fun! What exhilaration! What glitter! What a draw! And then . . . it's gone. Passed. Done. Confetti becomes litter, songs trail to silence, and the attraction of the crowd dwindles and dies.

This is how Marian Jordan describes her life without Jesus Christ. Fun, loud, colorful, cyclical . . . lonely and trashed. Her sharp observations of the party years resonate with the familiar. Her transparent account of the lure of fashion, sex, booze, and approval chronicles the dilemma of the "every girl" in today's society.

Marian's powerful testimony of coming to brokenness and emptiness and her dynamic account of the gentle mercy and forceful grace of Christ who called her into his arms permeate all of her writings and speaking engagements. Whole in Christ and ready to tell any ear that will listen, Marian has a passion for young women who flock to the parade of emptiness.

She is a dynamic speaker who leaves indelible marks on her audience . . . painful rib cages from laughter, and mind-searing impressions of being so-dead-on to one's private dilemmas. Marian has the gift of applying sound Biblical truth to the tender wounds of bleeding hearts. The girl can teach. The girl can relate. And the girl can move a wounded heart to change through an introduction to Jesus Christ, the Lord and Lover of her soul.

Today Marian, the founder of Redeemed Girl Ministries, is an active speaker, guest lecturer, and published author. She is a graduate of Southwestern Seminary and lives in Houston where she serves at her home church, Second Baptist Church of Houston when not on the road at speaking engagements. Though she is a Texas girl at heart, she feels at home in destinations all over the world. Australia, Costa Rica, Italy, England, Texas, or New York . . . she finds God's beauty in every country, city, and small town she happens upon. So now, when she does come across a parade, she can soak in the excitement and walk away content, knowing that the Master of Ceremonies will go with her to the next town, the next country, the next season of life. And that, friends, is the beauty of being a Redeemed Girl.

Please visit www.redeemedgirl.org or www.marianjordan.com for Marian's blog, speaking calendar, and resources.

Other B&H books by Marian Jordan

Sex and the City Uncovered: Exposing the Emptiness and Healing the Hurt

Wilderness Skills for Women: How to Survive Heartbreak and Other Full-Blown Meltdowns

Notes

Number 1—Shine

1. James Montgomery, reporting by Kim Stolz, "Pussycat Dolls Prepare for MTV Movie Awards Performance," www.mtv.com/movies/news/articles/1588426/20080530/story.jhtml, May 31, 2008.

2. John Piper, *Don't Waste Your Life* (Downers Grove, IL: Crossway, 2003), 31.

3. The first statement in the Westminster Shorter Catechism, considered a doctrinal statement written during the English Reformation. The purpose of the Shorter Catechism was to educate laypersons' children and new converts in doctrine and belief. For example: The question: "What is the chief end of man?" Answer: "To glorify God and enjoy Him forever."

4. Case in point, a girl may feel "happy" when she criticizes another person because she now feels superior and better about herself by putting someone else down. The problem is that this activity is unloving and therefore does not glorify God. While

she may temporarily feel "good" she will ultimately feel the consequences of sin and her life will not shine for God.

Number 2—Hope

1. *Concise Oxford Dictionary, 10th Edition*, Oxford University Press, 2001.

2. Anderson Cooper, *Dispatches from the Edge: A Memoir of War, Disasters, and Survival* (Harper Collins, 2006), 14.

Number 3—Pursue Beauty

1. *Mean Girls*, directed by Mark Waters (2004 Paramount Pictures, Hollywood, CA).

2. The American Society for Aesthetic Plastic Surgery, August 20, 2008, www.surgery.org.

3. For a daily quiet time guide see "Beautiful Time Tips" in the appendix.

4. *Turn Your Eyes upon Jesus*. Text and music by Helen H. Lemmel 1922.

Number 4—Seek First

1. John Piper, *Don't Waste Your Life* (Downers Grove, IL: Crossway, 2003), 35.

2. Quote by Mack Douglas found on www.thinkexist.com.

3. Rick Warren, *The Purpose Driven Life* (Grand Rapids, MI: Zondervan, 2002).

Number 5—Dance

1. *Sex and the City Uncovered*, Marian Jordan (Nashville, TN: B&H Publishing Group, 2007), 174–75.

2. Rick Warren, *The Purpose Driven Life* (Grand Rapids, MI: Zondervan, 2002), 83.

Beautiful Time Tips

1. I learned of the R.E.A.P. method from a sermon by Pastor Matt Carter from the Austin Stone Community Church in Austin, Texas.